International Relations: A Very Short Introduction

VERY SHORT INTRODUCTIONS are for anyone wanting a stimulating and accessible way in to a new subject. They are written by experts, and have been published in more than 25 languages worldwide.

The series began in 1995, and now represents a wide variety of topics in history, philosophy, religion, science, and the humanities. The VSI Library now contains over 200 volumes—a Very Short Introduction to everything from ancient Egypt and Indian philosophy to conceptual art and cosmology—and will continue to grow to a library of around 300 titles.

Very Short Introductions available now:

ADVERTISING Winston Fletcher
AFRICAN HISTORY John Parker and
    Richard Rathbone
AGNOSTICISM Robin Le Poidevin
AMERICAN POLITICAL PARTIES AND
    ELECTIONS L. Sandy Maisel
THE AMERICAN PRESIDENCY
    Charles O. Jones
ANARCHISM Colin Ward
ANCIENT EGYPT Ian Shaw
ANCIENT PHILOSOPHY Julia Annas
ANCIENT WARFARE Harry Sidebottom
ANGLICANISM Mark Chapman
THE ANGLO-SAXON AGE John Blair
ANIMAL RIGHTS David DeGrazia
ANTISEMITISM Steven Beller
THE APOCRYPHAL GOSPELS
    Paul Foster
ARCHAEOLOGY Paul Bahn
ARCHITECTURE Andrew Ballantyne
ARISTOCRACY William Doyle
ARISTOTLE Jonathan Barnes
ART HISTORY Dana Arnold
ART THEORY Cynthia Freeland
ATHEISM Julian Baggini
AUGUSTINE Henry Chadwick
AUTISM Uta Frith
BARTHES Jonathan Culler
BESTSELLERS John Sutherland
THE BIBLE John Riches
BIBLICAL ARCHEOLOGY Eric H. Cline
BIOGRAPHY Hermione Lee
THE BLUES Elijah Wald
THE BOOK OF MORMON Terryl Givens
THE BRAIN Michael O'Shea

BRITISH POLITICS Anthony Wright
BUDDHA Michael Carrithers
BUDDHISM Damien Keown
BUDDHIST ETHICS Damien Keown
CAPITALISM James Fulcher
CATHOLICISM Gerald O'Collins
THE CELTS Barry Cunliffe
CHAOS Leonard Smith
CHOICE THEORY Michael Allingham
CHRISTIAN ART Beth Williamson
CHRISTIAN ETHICS D. Stephen Long
CHRISTIANITY Linda Woodhead
CITIZENSHIP Richard Bellamy
CLASSICAL MYTHOLOGY Helen Morales
CLASSICS Mary Beard and John Henderson
CLAUSEWITZ Michael Howard
THE COLD WAR Robert McMahon
COMMUNISM Leslie Holmes
CONSCIOUSNESS Susan Blackmore
CONTEMPORARY ART Julian Stallabrass
CONTINENTAL PHILOSOPHY
    Simon Critchley
COSMOLOGY Peter Coles
THE CRUSADES Christopher Tyerman
CRYPTOGRAPHY Fred Piper and
    Sean Murphy
DADA AND SURREALISM David Hopkins
DARWIN Jonathan Howard
THE DEAD SEA SCROLLS Timothy Lim
DEMOCRACY Bernard Crick
DESCARTES Tom Sorell
DESERTS Nick Middleton
DESIGN John Heskett
DINOSAURS David Norman
DIPLOMACY Joseph M. Siracusa

For more information visit our web site:
www.oup.co.uk/general/vsi/

Paul Wilkinson

INTERNATIONAL RELATIONS

A Very Short Introduction

OXFORD
UNIVERSITY PRESS

OXFORD

UNIVERSITY PRESS

Great Clarendon Street, Oxford OX2 6DP

Oxford University Press is a department of the University of Oxford.
It furthers the University's objective of excellence in research, scholarship,
and education by publishing worldwide in

Oxford New York

Auckland Cape Town Dar es Salaam Hong Kong Karachi
Kuala Lumpur Madrid Melbourne Mexico City Nairobi
New Delhi Shanghai Taipei Toronto

With offices in

Argentina Austria Brazil Chile Czech Republic France Greece
Guatemala Hungary Italy Japan Poland Portugal Singapore
South Korea Switzerland Thailand Turkey Ukraine Vietnam

Oxford is a registered trade mark of Oxford University Press
in the UK and in certain other countries

Published in the United States
by Oxford University Press Inc., New York

© Paul Wilkinson 2007

The moral rights of the author have been asserted

Database right Oxford University Press (maker)

First published as a Very Short Introduction 2007

British Library Cataloguing in Publication Data

Data available

Library of Congress Cataloging in Publication Data

Data available

ISBN 978–0–19–280157–9

7 9 10 8

Typeset by SPI Publisher Services, Pondicherry, India
Printed in Great Britain by
Ashford Colour Press Ltd, Gosport, Hampshire

For my grandchildren:
James, Rebecca, Molly, Amy, Jack, Lola, Lois and Nell

Contents

List of illustrations

Introduction

What is this book about?

International relations is a very broad concept. In modern usage
it includes not only relations between states but also between
states and non-state organizations such as churches,
humanitarian relief organizations and multinational corporations,
and between states and intergovernmental organizations (IGOs),
such as the UN and the EU. In this very brief introduction I shall
be using this broad concept of the subject.

The subject of international relations is taught in many
universities, often in combination with, or as part of, the
curriculum of political science. But in my view the attempt by
political scientists to exert some kind of monopoly over the
subject of international relations is neither practicable nor
sustainable. The serious student of international relations
needs to have some knowledge of international history, law,
and economics as well as foreign policy and international
politics.

It is the complex and multidisciplinary nature of the subject
that has made the search for an effective general theory of
international relations 'mission impossible'. This is not to say that
valuable partial or limited theories applicable to certain

aspects of the subject do not exist. (For example, there are useful bodies of theory on international development, arms control, trade cycles, and arms races). But the main schools of general theory of international relations are not proven in any scientific sense: rather they constitute ways of perceiving international relations, metaphors or models which appeal to their adherents because that is the way they prefer to view the world. It could be argued that if a particular approach to interpreting international relations becomes sufficiently widely held it could become self-fulfilling. A good example of this is realist theory of international relations, still arguably the most influential school of thought in international relations on both sides of the Atlantic.

Realist theory

The true precursors of the modern realist school of thought in international relations were Niccolo Machiavelli, author of *The Prince* (1532), and Thomas Hobbes, who wrote *The Leviathan* (1651), for both of these political philosophers assumed that human beings were fundamentally motivated by their own self-interests and appetites and that the most widespread and potentially dangerous of all these appetites is their lust for power. In their view, the sovereign who rules the state is the true and only guarantor of internal peace because he alone has power to enforce the peace. However, in the wider world of international politics the law of the jungle applied.

In their view, international politics was a constant struggle for power, not necessarily resulting in constant open warfare, but always necessitating a readiness to go to war. In this continual state of anarchy the only prudent course for the prince was to accumulate as much power as possible and to use that power to defend and pursue their national interest. For this purpose military power was the key requirement: wealth from commerce and industry were seen mainly as a means to acquiring the necessary military power.

1. Niccolo Machiavelli (1469–1527), secretary to the War Council of the Republic of Forence (1498–1512) and political philosopher. In *The Prince* (1532) he provided a candid and amoral guide on how to seize and maintain power over a state.

Modern realists accept, explicitly or implicitly, these underlying assumptions, and stress the continuing necessity of alliance-building, the role of the state as key political actor, the maintenance of a favourable balance of power, and a firm refusal to entrust security to international organizations and agreements, as essential components of an effective national security policy.

It is clear that the realist approach to international relations will tend to appeal to those of a very conservative and pessimistic disposition who take a pretty dim view of human nature and have little or no faith in liberal institution building, international law, or any moves towards regional integration or world governance through world organizations.

These ideas dominated the thinking of US and West European political leaders during the cold war. Not surprisingly, there are many academics, politicians, and citizens who take a very different view.

Liberal institutionalism and interdependence

Interdependence theory developed as a critique of realist theory in the 1970s. It challenged the realist idea that the state was the most important entity in international relations. Interdependence theorists stressed the importance of non-state actors, such as multinational corporations and their influential role in a more complex global society in which military power had become far less important or virtually irrelevant to shaping relations between countries. Liberal institutionalist and interdependence approaches overlap to a considerable extent. Both have a much more optimistic view of human nature and share the view that growing interdependence will strengthen the institutions of regional cooperation and open up greater opportunities for strengthening the United Nations and developing mechanisms of world governance.

It is certainly possible for the liberal institutionalists to point to the fact that the overwhelming majority of transactions between states are peaceful, in accordance with international law, and to the mutual benefit of the states involved. The creation and development of the European Union can be seen from the liberal perspective as a powerful riposte to those who believe international politics is based on nothing more than a constant pursuit of power after power and that it always must be a zero-sum game.

Postmodern deconstructionism

Postmodern deconstructionists are participants in a broader philosophical movement called critical social theory. They claim to be able to 'deconstruct' the writings and discourse of academics and policy makers who interpret the world, including, of course, international relations. They believe that they are able, by the process of 'deconstruction', to uncover the underlying 'subjective' meanings and intentions of the texts in the light of the social and cultural climate in which they were produced. Their depressing conclusion is that there is no objective international truth or reality we can discover. Hence, instead of studying the real world of international relations they spend their time trying to reveal what they believe to be the 'distortions', 'subtexts', and 'deceptive' use of language in the texts in the 'conventional' literature. Paradoxically, the critical theorists who claim to use these methods spend all their time criticizing the authors of the texts, and have little or nothing to offer by way of independent criticism of the actual policies and actions of policy makers, either in their own countries or internationally – a clear case of self-destruction?

The need for common sense on the role of theory

There are many other theoretical approaches to the study of international relations but I am not going to take up the reader's time with a long list. It is not the case that I am opposed to theory. On the contrary, the search for a solid body of theory which can be empirically validated and which really does help us to explain key phenomena in international relations is a central task of scholarship in all subjects. However, I do urge the reader to maintain a healthy scepticism in appraising attempts at general (sometimes termed 'grand') theory – which on close examination is riddled with unsubstantiated sweeping generalizations, the creation of *grands simplificateurs*.

This book will introduce concepts, metaphors, and models and some partial theories where I think they will help the newcomer to international relations. However, my main aim is to provide a brief introduction to the complexities and problems of the real world of international relations. The suggested further readings at the end of the book provide many different perspectives on theory. As the well-informed reader will discover, I am not afraid to enter the normative theory debate. One of the reasons why the study of international relations is so attractive to thoughtful students is that it inevitably raises so many complex ethical issues. I have been criticized for my liberal views on my subject. I see no reason to apologize and I have no doubt that many readers will disagree with my opinions on how statesmen, governments, and IGOs ought to guide us to a better and more peaceful future. I can assure my critics that I do not for one moment underestimate the difficulty of the task.

Anatomy of an international crisis

The conflicts which erupted on 13 June and 12 July 2006 between Israel, on the one hand, and Palestinian militants in Gaza and the Lebanese Shi'ite movement Hezbollah, on the other, had many similarities to the Israeli invasion of Lebanon in 1982. The trigger for the launch of the invasion was the assassination attempt on the Israeli Ambassador in London, Shlomo Argov. The terrorists responsible for the shooting of Ambassador Argov were from the Abu Nidal Organization, a group bitterly opposed to the Palestine Liberation Organization (PLO) and its leader, Yasser Arafat. Neither the Lebanese civilians nor the PLO were responsible for the attack on Mr Argov but the Israeli government nevertheless launched a massive assault on Lebanon. Their real motivation was to reshape Lebanese politics permanently by ensuring that a government compliant with Israeli policies was installed and that Palestinian militants would no longer be able to use Lebanon as a base from which they could attack Israel.

The war led to a prolonged Israeli siege of Beirut which inflicted huge suffering and destruction on Lebanese civilians. Ariel Sharon and Israeli military officers were accused of standing aside and allowing Lebanese Phalangists to massacre Palestinian refugees in camps in Sabra and Chatilla. Israel lost a great deal of international support because Israel's military bombardment of Lebanon was seen to be totally disproportionate in relation to the alleged justification for the invasion. Israel failed dismally in its attempt to insert a pro-Israeli government in Lebanon and created so much hatred and resentment among the Shi'ites of South Lebanon that it mobilized mass support for a new militant Shi'ite insurgent movement, Hezbollah (the 'Party of God'), which has been a thorn in Israel's side ever since. The only 'success' Israel achieved from its invasion of Lebanon was the evacuation of Arafat and the PLO factions to Tunisia. What the 1982 invasion showed, above all, was the inability of even a powerfully armed state like Israel to defeat terrorism by the use of massive military force, and the inability of the international community to intervene rapidly enough to prevent large-scale suffering and killing of civilians.

The conflict which erupted in the summer of 2006 once again provides a tragic demonstration of the capacity of states to have a disproportionate reaction to acts of terrorism and to escalate to the level of terror wars, causing infinitely more death and destruction than they are supposed to be countering. Moreover, in the case of Israel and its Palestinian and Lebanese opponents it is by no means always straightforward to decide who initiated each new cycle of terror and counter-terror. In all the focus on Lebanon by the media in July 2006 many have overlooked the fact that the original trigger for the escalation to a new war was the shelling of a beach in Gaza by the Israelis which killed seven members of a Palestinian family.

Hamas, which had defeated Fatah in the Palestinian elections in January 2006, and which had observed a military truce with Israel since March 2005, called off its ceasefire in response to the shelling of the Gaza beach. On 13 June a Palestinian family of nine was killed in an Israeli missile strike on Gaza. This was the context in which Palestinian militants mounted a cross-border raid into Israel, kidnapping an Israeli soldier and killing two others. When the Palestinian militants refused to release the Israeli soldier, Israel took draconian action, bombarding Gaza from the air and detaining Hamas cabinet members and legislators. Hezbollah, which has long made common cause with the Palestinians against Israel, then provoked conflict with Israel on the Northern front by capturing two Israeli soldiers and killing eight others.

It was in its response to these serious terrorist incidents that Israel launched a massive air bombardment of Lebanon on 14 July. Although Israel's avowed purpose was to eradicate Hezbollah and to destroy its supply of rockets and rocket launchers capable of hitting not only villagers across the border in Northern Israel but also of reaching civilian targets in Haifa, the Israeli air bombardment hit at a far wider range of targets and killed and injured hundreds of innocent civilians, including large numbers of children. Moreover, by its blockade of Lebanese ports and its bombing of Beirut Airport, Israel made it extremely difficult for international humanitarian aid to reach the civilian population. Small wonder that the Lebanese prime minister called urgently for a ceasefire and described his country as a 'disaster zone'.

Sadly, however, calls for the belligerents to exercise restraint were largely ignored, just as they have been in the conflicts of Iraq, Central Africa, the former Yugoslavia, Chechnya, and many other areas. UN officials did their best to remind the belligerents of their responsibilities under international humanitarian law. After touring a bombed neighbourhood of South Beirut, Jan Egeland, emergency relief coordinator for the UN, stated:

> Bombing civilian populations is wrong, destroying civilian infrastructure is wrong... It is wrong also for Hezbollah to continue firing rockets against Israeli towns.... Civilian populations are not targets. That is against the law, humanitarian law.

Louise Arbour, the UN High Commissioner for Human Rights said: 'What I've tried to do is to remind those who under international criminal law may incur personal criminal responsibility for these actions'.

Sadly, these warnings once again fell on deaf ears. Israel was even able to score a direct hit on a UN Observer (UNIFIL) post in South Lebanon killing four UN personnel, with apparent impunity. As will be made clear later in this book, it is not much good having a body of international law to protect human rights if this is repeatedly violated. Lebanese civilians were in the true sense the hapless innocent victims of Israeli bombardment. Their government had no advance warning of the Hezbollah seizure of Israeli soldiers. Hezbollah operates more like a state within a state, and the fragile recently emerged Lebanese democratically elected government lacked the military strength to regain control of South Lebanon from Hezbollah, or to prevent Hezbollah attacks on Israel.

What of the international diplomatic efforts to try to resolve the crisis? Once again, as will be argued later in this *Very Short Introduction to International Relations*, the diplomacy of crisis management and war prevention was hampered by the unilateral neo-conservative foreign policy stance of President George W. Bush's administration, and by deep divisions among the regional powers in zones of conflict. In the case of the Middle East crisis of summer 2006, the apparent total support for Israel on the part of the US, supported by Prime Minister Tony Blair, seriously damaged Washington's chances of emerging as a credible peace-maker in the conflict. A UN Security Council resolution calling on Israel to withdraw from Gaza was vetoed by the US. At the G8 Conference in St Petersburg, President Bush, supported by Mr Blair, blocked the call for an immediate ceasefire voiced by other leaders. And the US Secretary of State's call for a 'new Middle East' and an 'enduring peace' was at first rejected by Lebanon and by Hezbollah when it emerged that Ms Rice was making such a peace conditional on meeting all Israeli's major objectives, i.e. disarming Hezbollah, placing an international force in South Lebanon to act as a buffer against any security threat to Israel, and the immediate release of the captured Israeli soldiers without reciprocal release of Israeli-held prisoners.

At the time of writing it was still unclear how this crisis would evolve. It seemed unlikely that the Olmert government of Israel would abandon its efforts to eradicate the Hezbollah problem from its northern border. The efforts of some able diplomats to obtain a diplomatic settlement did ultimately bear fruit, and a ceasefire was achieved in mid-August 2006 but if it breaks down there would be tragic consequences for the civilian population and, in the worst case, a widening into a conflict involving Iran and Syria.

A major lesson of the conflict in Lebanon in July–August 2006 is that air bombardment, however intensive, is not an effective or morally legitimate means of trying to eradicate a threat from a non-state guerrilla or terrorist group. Another, very disappointing lesson that should be drawn is that, just as has been demonstrated in the Iraq conflict, a country that has prided itself on being a democracy, once it starts using terror to defeat terror, is fully capable of violating human rights and committing war crimes and thus losing the moral high ground.

The dangerous Middle East crisis of the summer of 2006, in my view, underlines the urgent need for imaginative and creative international statesmanship and for more effective diplomacy of conflict management. An important yet constantly neglected precondition for more effective diplomacy of crisis management and conflict termination is a far greater knowledge and understanding of how other states and non-states, and especially those who oppose our own states, perceive the world and the disputes and conflicts in which they are involved. One is unlikely to win battles of 'hearts and minds' if one has no understanding of the way other states, societies, and non-state organizations see us and the rest of the world. Hence, we also need greater understanding of the roles and capabilities of states, non-states, and intergovernmental organizations and of the profound global problems and challenges we all confront. This short book aims to provide an overview of the main actors in international relations and some of their most intractable problems.

Chapter 1
States

Let us imagine a newly appointed US Secretary of State being briefed by a senior adviser on her first day in office.

In the US system, unlike the UK, there is a role for the Senate which has to formally approve of any new appointment to the post of Secretary of State and it would be the normal expectation that the appointee would be able to satisfy the Senate regarding their expertise and experience in dealing with foreign affairs. In Britain's parliamentary democracy the only qualification needed for appointment as Foreign Secretary is the willingness of the Prime Minister to offer you the job. In some cases, Prime Ministers prefer to take all key foreign policy decisions themselves or with their 'kitchen cabinet' of unelected personal advisers. In these circumstances, the Foreign Secretary's job will simply be to implement the Prime Minister's policies. In any event, and whatever the personal relations of the Prime Minister with his Foreign Secretary, and even if both these politicians are new to foreign affairs, the senior officials at the Foreign and Commonwealth Office have such a combined weight of knowledge and experience derived from service in diplomatic posts all over the world that they can more than compensate for weaknesses at ministerial levels. Under the US system the State Department has a similar wealth of expertise, but again may find that the President's main interest is in foreign affairs and that the Secretary of State is expected simply to implement loyally White House policy. A complication of the US system is that rival departments, especially the Department of Defense and the National Security Council, may disagree with the State Department and seek to promote their own preferred policy.

One of the first things a very inexperienced new UK Foreign Secretary will need to be briefed about is states, for we live in a world in which states are still the key actors in international relations. As there is no world government and no system of world law and law enforcement, and no sign of any such systems being established, knowledge of states is likely to remain a necessary, though of course not a sufficient, requirement for any serious understanding of international relations for the foreseeable future. It is mere wishful thinking to pretend otherwise.

It was not always thus. Anthropologists have described in fascinating detail human societies based on tribal or clan membership where nothing resembling a state existed (Margaret Mead, *Coming of Age in Samoa*, 1929, for example). In such societies, which still survive in places such as Central Africa and the Central Amazon basin, there are certainly tribal rulers or chieftains and elders but there are no full-time officials and in many cases, because tribes can be nomadic, there is no fixed territory with recognized borders or tribal jurisdiction. It is in the ancient empires of Egypt, Persia, China, and Rome that we find some of the key characteristics of the state emerging. Rulers employ retinues of officials to implement and enforce their decrees. Armies of full-time soldiers are deployed for the purposes of further imperial conquests and to repel external and internal enemies. Often quite complex legal codes and criminal justice procedures are developed and employed (with varying degrees of efficiency and consistency) throughout the territories of the empire. One only has to consider the huge influence of

Roman law on the legal systems of contemporary Europe to see the importance of these developments for the emergence of the modern state.

At the opposite end of the spectrum so far as scale is concerned were the small city-states of ancient Greece, so brilliantly caught in Aristotle's *Politics*, and the Italian city-states of the early modern period. In his classic writings on the latter, Niccolo Machiavelli provides a fascinating realist insight into the strategies and tactics used by the successful Prince or ruler to seize and retain power and the techniques of statecraft needed to conduct a successful foreign policy in the constant power struggles and rivalries between different city-states, principalities, and republics of Renaissance Italy. In the Italian city-states of this period we should note one of the most important precursors of the modern state: the growing assertion of the secular over the religious life.

Indeed it is with the Reformation in Europe and the clear and irrevocable separation of church and state that the conditions emerge for the development of a truly modern state system in Europe in which no single state is recognized as the legitimate hegemony or dominant power, and in which all member states *in principle* agree to mutually recognize each other's right to sovereign rights and jurisdiction over their own territories.

The true beginning of the modern state system in Europe was the Peace of Westphalia (1648) which marked the end of the Thirty Years War. The war had not simply been a struggle between Catholicism and Calvinism. It was an international conflict between the Holy Roman Empire and the powerful sovereign states such as France, which sought to ensure that they obtained strategic and defensive frontiers. The power and authority of the Holy Roman Empire was drastically curtailed by the Peace of Westphalia.

The sovereign authority of the Austrian Habsburgs (traditionally the family from which the Holy Roman Emperor had been elected) was effectively restricted to their hereditary Austrian duchies and Bohemia. The empire was no longer permitted to raise troops, declare war or make peace, or raise taxes without the consent of the members of the state system. And the 300 or so states into which Germany was divided became true states in the modern sense: that is to say they were recognized as sovereign independent states and were therefore free to form alliances with other states not only within but also outwith the imperial league. Moreover the essentially secular basis of the new state system was strongly reaffirmed when the principle, *Cujus regio, ejus religio* (Such government in a state, such religion in a state) first enunciated at Augsburg in 1555, was enshrined in the Peace of Westphalia and extended to cover Calvinism in addition to Lutheranism. Henceforth, the major inter-state conflicts in Europe were about power and territory and not about seeking religious dominance. The state, the basic unit of our modern global state system, is a complex political and legal concept of crucial importance in the study of international relations. According to international law, all states have a legal personality and even the smallest and least powerful state has to meet certain basic criteria in order to obtain recognition as a member of the state system by other states in the global system of states. It must have a defined territory, a permanent population, and a government which is capable of maintaining effective control over its territory and conducting international relations with other states.

In the real world of international relations there is enormous variation in the degree to which states meet these criteria. For example, many states struggle to maintain effective sovereign control over even part of their defined territory. Many states do not have a monopoly of control of armed force within their frontiers and find themselves confronted by civil wars and insurgents, which leave whole areas of their countries under the control of rebel leaders and war lords (for example, Afghanistan, Angola, Burma, Colombia, Somalia, and Sudan). Yet despite experiencing such fundamental challenges to their sovereignty such states still receive international recognition, sign agreements with other states, send delegates to the United Nations and other international bodies, and enjoy the outward (if only symbolic) appearance of full membership of the global community of states, now numbering almost 200.

Even external recognition is not an absolute criterion of statehood. For decades US governments withheld diplomatic recognition from communist China, and many countries refused to recognize the state of Israel. Thus it is clear that external recognition does not have to be universally accorded before the status of statehood can be achieved. Generally we can say that it is enough to have external recognition from a considerable number of states, including most major powers, and most important of all, from the United Nations. Recognition by the United Nations is today the sine qua non of achieving full statehood.

The term 'nation-state' is often used to designate the state as described above. This is helpful for two main reasons: (i) it immediately differentiates the states which are sovereign and part of the global states system from those which are, in effect, units of regional or local government within sovereign states, such as the states that comprise the United States or the State of Amazonas in Brazil or the State of Tamil Nadu in south-east India; and (ii) almost all sovereign states, even those which comprise a variety of ethnic and religious groups, seek to foster a sense of national identity and loyalty which is coterminous with the entire population and hence it is possible to observe an Indian nationalism which transcends local loyalties, an American nationalism which, despite the 'melting pot' of diverse origins of the population, instils a fierce loyalty to the Union, and in the United Kingdom, which is comprised of English, Scottish, Welsh, Northern Irish, Afro-Caribbean, and other ethnic identities, there is still a strong current of British nationalism rooted in a shared monarchy, a common central government, and long experience of close political, economic, and social interaction in times of peace and war.

It is obvious from the maps of multi-ethnic states such as Russia, India, Nigeria, Indonesia, and Myanmar (formerly Burma) that it would be foolish to assume that states and nations are coterminous. Many ethnic minorities are ruled by states they never chose to join, some (for example, the Kurds in the Middle East) have found their populations divided by political frontiers created in the period of European colonization, only to be reaffirmed by new elites in the decolonization process. Hence, although the 'nation-state' is in common usage and almost every state in the global states system engages in some form of 'nation-building' activity, we should be aware that there is a huge amount of tension, hostility, and outright conflict between 'state' and 'nation' in modern international relations. It is just as important for us to study non-state movements, such as separatist groups and national liberation movements, as it is to investigate the policies and activities of the states which so often find themselves challenged by these phenomena. Accepting the reality that states are the most significant and influential units in the global international system does *not* imply that international relations should be studied in a purely state-centric mode. To do so would be to fall into one of the most serious errors of recent so-called international relations theory. I will return to some of these problems in Chapter 3.

The limits of the US superpower

Since the implosion of the Former Soviet Union in 1989–90, the United States has been the world's only superpower, and the Secretary of State's adviser will remind her that the US greatly valued the support of NATO allies in the cold war and will hardly need to stress the importance of maintaining the 'special relationship' with the UK born in the Second World War alliance and close relations with the other NATO alliance countries, which continued throughout the cold war and into the post-cold war era.

Statistics on the world economy show that the US has by far the biggest economy, with a GDP over twice the size of its nearest rival and the greatest purchasing power of any state. It also has the largest inventory of nuclear weapons and the most advanced high-tech weaponry in the world. America's superpower status depends on this vital continuation of huge economic strength and incredibly high levels of military expenditure, only made possible by America's unique wealth. Moreover, as demonstrated convincingly in the conflicts in the Balkans and in the Middle East since the end of the cold war, the US has a unique capability for the rapid deployment of its forces deploying both airlift and sealift assets with remarkable speed.

Hence, what differentiates the US from other major powers in purely military terms is not just their unrivalled investment on research and development for the military, but also their ability to *project* military power into any part of the world with unrivalled speed.

Our newly installed Foreign Secretary, on the other hand, will constantly be reminded by his senior officials and advisers of the importance of maintaining and, where possible, strengthening the 'special relationship' with the US. The Minister will be made aware of the enormous assets the US brings to the North Atlantic Alliance and the damage that would be inflicted on British interests around the world if the relationship with the US were to be put at risk through British failure to act in accord with US foreign policy. The Suez Crisis of 1956, when Prime Minister Anthony Eden conspired with the French and Israelis to invade Egypt with the aim of forcing Nasser to rescind his decision to nationalize the Suez Canal, provoked an angry response from the then US President, Dwight Eisenhower and his Secretary of

State, John Foster Dulles. They threatened to pull the plug on the pound sterling. Eden was forced to resign. In the eyes of the British establishment a key lesson of the Suez Crisis was that, in the words of Tony Judt in his excellent study, *Postwar*: 'the UK must never again put itself on the wrong side of an argument with Washington'.

However, a wise Permanent Under-Secretary with a good knowledge of recent history should surely caution against the idea that the UK should automatically fall in with the wishes of its most powerful ally. There is a difference between mere subservience and genuine alliance. The UK is an independent sovereign state and British national interests do not always coincide with those of the US. If Britain had blindly followed US foreign policy when Hitler invaded Poland the Nazis might well have succeeded in occupying the whole of Europe before the US woke from its isolationist slumbers. It would have been a total catastrophe. In more recent history we have the interesting example of Prime Minister Harold Wilson who turned down US requests that Britain provide military contributions to assist them in their war in Vietnam. The British government's decision to abstain from that tragic and protracted war turned out to be extremely wise. It took the US years to extricate from that unwinnable conflict, and Americans paid a huge price in terms of lives lost and treasure expended. Vietnam suffered huge loss of life of soldiers and civilians on both sides and huge economic destruction. Cambodia, which provided convenient routes for the North to move troops and military equipment to the South, also suffered much destruction from massive US aerial bombardment.

In embarking on the invasion of Iraq in March 2003, the US leaders appear to have entirely forgotten the lessons of their recent history. They appear to have really believed the claims of Iraqi exiles that the people of Iraq would greet the US troops as liberators and garland them with flowers. The White House and the Pentagon did not allow for the possibility of serious and prolonged resistance to the US occupation and chose to take no notice of warning from the State Department, the CIA, and other parts of the US government where there was expert knowledge on Iraq and the Middle East generally. This tells us a great deal about the importance of well informed leadership in foreign policy and the need to utilize expert judgement in decision making.

It is even more extraordinary that Prime Minister Tony Blair pledged unhesitating and unconditional support for the plan to invade Iraq and that large numbers of British troops found themselves deployed to Iraq where their major task was to maintain order in Basra and the Shi'ite region of Southern Iraq. Both President Bush and Prime Minister Blair claim to have embarked on the invasion in Iraq in good faith. President Bush and his neo-conservative advisers told the American public that Saddam Hussein had been involved in the 9/11 attacks on the World Trade Center and the Pentagon. Prime Minster Tony Blair told the British Parliament that Saddam had weapons of mass destruction (WMD) and that his missiles posed a threat to the United Kingdom. Both these justifications turned out to be entirely bogus, and by spring 2006 sizeable majorities of the US and UK populations opposed their governments' policies on Iraq. By May 2007 over 64,000 civilians had been killed in the conflict in Iraq, in addition to over 3,400 US servicemen and 148 UK military.

Perhaps, the most important lesson that the US government and the rest of the international community should draw from the searing experience of the invasion and occupation of Iraq, and from the 9/11 attacks, concerns the *limits* of superpower. Even a great power with all the resources and global military reach of the US cannot control the entire political and strategic environment. In circumstances sadly reminiscent of the Vietnam War, the US has proved unable to secure its strategic objects even when confronted with relatively small wars and insurgencies. Just as the US governments of Richard Nixon and Lyndon Johnson were unable to secure the survival of a non-communist state in South Vietnam, it appears that the Bush administration is not going to be able to suppress the insurgency in Iraq or to prevent that country from descending into the nightmare of all-out civil war. From a strategic perspective one clear lesson is that the war in Iraq has been counterproductive in the struggle against Al Qaeda. The invasion was an ideological and propaganda gift to the Al Qaeda network of networks. It provided them with more recruits, more donations from wealthy Muslims, and a tempting array of military and civilian targets from coalition countries just across the borders of states where they have many militants and sympathizers. When Iraq was invaded in March 2003 it was a hostile area for Al Qaeda. Saddam Hussein was ideologically and politically the kind of leader that bin Laden and his followers loved to hate. Now, Iraq has become a major base for Al Qaeda and it is clear from the propaganda messages of bin Laden and his deputy, Zawahiri, that Al Qaeda is making a major effort to derail the fragile new Iraqi government and to establish a base in Iraq from which to launch terrorist attacks on neighbouring regimes, for example, in Jordan and Saudi Arabia, which they allege are 'Apostate' regimes because of their cooperation with the West and refusal to follow the 'true Islam' as proclaimed by bin Laden and his followers.

US superpower has serious limits not only because of the way it can overstretch its military and economic resources but also because it often lacks the quality of political leadership and statesmanship that would enable it to deal more successfully with its big security challenges, and to manage conflict and crisis situations effectively without rushing to resorting to war at the first opportunity. Many of the limits on the US superpower are to a large extent self-inflicted, but they are all too real. If America's friends and allies recognize this there is a chance that they may be able to persuade the US government to adopt a more genuinely multilateral and multi-pronged strategic approach to foreign policy.

It is hardly surprising that the US superpower attracts a great deal of hostility in the international community. This has always been the fate of great powers. However, there is a big difference between general attitudes of anti-Americanism and support for terrorist attacks on Americans at home and abroad. It would surely make good sense to make one of the key foreign-policy aims the improvement of influence and friendly relations with the majority populations in the Muslim world and also more widely.

A change towards 'civilian' foreign policy by the US, using the 'soft power' of trade, aid, and cultural, scientific, and technological cooperation would do much to dissipate the image of a superpower reacting to challenges and problems in international relations with a heavy-handed over-reliance on military power and intervention.

US foreign policy, 9/11, and the swing to unilateralism

During George W. Bush's presidential election contest with Al Gore and in the early days of President Bush's first term, it appeared that the new administration intended to retreat from the global activism and intervention policies followed by President Clinton. George W. Bush won the election by the narrowest of margins after a campaign fought almost entirely on domestic issues.

It was the events of 11 September 2001 which led to George W. Bush declaring a War on Terror, transforming his foreign policy into one of global power projection and interventionism on a scale not seen since the height of the cold war confrontation with the Soviet Union. 9/11 gave the President's posse of neo-conservative advisers a golden opportunity to provide the White House with a new foreign-policy agenda which was a radical departure from the foreign policies of multilateralism and conflict management mediated through the United Nations. The American public

2. President George W. Bush declared a 'War on Terror' after 9/11. Al Qaeda had previously declared a 'global jihad' against the US and its allies.

was shocked by the scale of the death and destruction caused by the terrorist attacks on the World Trade Center and the Pentagon in which nearly 3,000 were killed, and by a new sense of vulnerability of the US homeland to what seemed to them to be a new kind of war. Hence, President Bush's declaration of a 'War on Terror' captured the public mood. There was a widespread yearning to strike back at America's perceived enemies (even if most Americans were not too sure who they were), and to restore national pride, a mood symbolized by the display of the American flag in the streets of every city and town and in the windows of thousands of private homes and businesses around the country.

The initial US response to 9/11 did not at first appear to presage a seismic shift in US foreign policy. The formation of the Coalition Against Terrorism and the swift actions of the UN Security Council, NATO, and OSCE in support of the US seemed to indicate a promising future for multilateral cooperation against the international terrorism of the Al Qaeda network. The swift

US military intervention in Afghanistan in collaboration with the Northern Alliance, which led to the overthrow of the Taliban regime, seemed justified in the eyes of most of the international community because, after all, the Taliban rulers had given safe haven and protection to bin Laden's Al Qaeda movement, the terrorist network responsible for planning and carrying out the 9/11 attacks.

But the neo-conservatives' project, which was adopted so readily by the President, was in reality far more ambitious. Their central idea was to use United States superpower capability – military and economic – to impose regime change and actively promote democracy and market economics. With hopeless overconfidence in their own power, reminiscent of the leaders of the British Empire in the Victorian era, the neo-conservatives appear to have believed that they could reshape the world in their own image. Clear evidence of the neo-conservatives' willingness to defy the norms of multilateralism and the constraints of the UN Charter and customary international law came with the US invasion and occupation of Iraq, carried out with the assistance of the UK government in defiance of the UN Security Council. The lurch towards unilateralism and aggressive nationalism on the part of the sole remaining superpower had serious consequences for international relations generally. Hopes of a concert of the major powers emerging in the UN Security Council to develop multilateral, political, and diplomatic solutions to problems of conflict in the post-cold war world were quickly dashed.

The US government introduced a new national security doctrine of pre-emptive military action to justify the invasion of Iraq. In reality, Iraq under the Saddam dictatorship did not constitute a threat to US security or even the security of the nearest neighbours in the Middle East. It was one of the most contained states in the world: it was subject to 'no-fly zones', it had been weakened by sanctions, and if the US had been willing to wait for

Dr Hans Blix, former chief UN weapons inspector in Iraq, and his weapons inspectors to finish their task in Iraq before the US/UK invasion, it would have been shown that the Iraqi regime did not have the weapons of mass destruction which the US and the UK governments claimed it had. The neo-conservatives' claims that Saddam was somehow involved in plotting the 9/11 attacks and that he was in league with bin Laden were sheer nonsense. The harsh truth is that President Bush and Prime Minister Blair, America's major ally and supporter in the invasion of Iraq, took their countries to war on a bogus prospectus. Who could deny that the Saddam regime was cruel tyranny and that it had committed major crimes against the Kurdish and Shi'ite populations of Iraq? But if we were to intervene in every dictatorship which violates human rights we would constantly be at war with brutal regimes all over the world.

A key lesson of the Iraq conflict is that political leaders should be made aware of the practical limitations and dangers of this pre-emptive military action doctrine. There are apparently some hard-line hawks who believe that a military intervention either by the US or Israel to destroy Iran's nuclear facilities would be justified because of the danger that Iran's successful enrichment of uranium may lead to the development of Iranian nuclear weapons. The hatred and desire for revenge that this would generate not only in Iran but in the Muslim world generally would almost certainly fuel an increase in international terrorism by jihadi groups around the world, just as the invasion and occupation of Iraq served as a huge propaganda boost and recruiting sergeant for the Al Qaeda network of networks. Quite apart from this, there is the danger of another war in the Middle East in which thousands more innocent civilians would be killed.

The increased danger of war and terrorism emanating from US foreign policy in the Middle East is of course only one manifestation of US unilateralism: unwillingness to sign up to the Kyoto agreement on the emission of greenhouse gases and to support the International Criminal Court, designed to deal with major crimes against humanity and war crimes, were also depressing evidence of the effects of arrogant nationalist rejections of multilateral cooperation to deal with major global problems.

The balance of power and the security dilemma

The weakening of multilateralism is by no means the fault of the US government alone. China has been pursuing its expansion of both its nuclear weapons programme and its conventional military forces with a single-mindedness that worries many of its neighbours. Russian foreign policy under President Putin has been characterized increasingly by revanchism, that is by the aim of regaining control, or at least dominance, over lost territories. Putin came to power in Russia partly on the promise that he would use Russian military force to prevent Chechnya from breaking away from the Russian Federation. More recently Putin's government has clashed openly with the Ukraine, doing its best to assist Mr Yushchenko's opponent in the Ukrainian elections and suspending gas sales and causing an energy crises not only in the Ukraine but in Europe generally. Putin has also supported two breakaway regions in Georgia, much to the fury of the authorities in Tbilisi. Growing hostility between Moscow and the governments of Azerbaijan, Armenia, Georgia, the Ukraine and Moldova, seem likely to lead to the break-up of the Commonwealth of Independent States (CIS), set up in 1991 as a framework for maintaining links between Russia and the newly independent states. Indeed in May 2006 it seemed likely that the pro-Western states of Georgia, Moldova, Azerbaijan, and the Ukraine would form their own regional organization to promote democratic values.

President Putin has also embarked on a major rearmament programme. The Russian government has clearly worried about the extension of NATO membership to embrace East European states and by the US decision to site anti-ballistic missiles in Eastern Europe.

What we are seeing in all these trends is evidence that, far from witnessing a strengthening of multilateral institutions and global political integration, what we are really seeing is the enduring reality of our system of independent sovereign states: rivalry and conflict between the major and even the medium and minor powers; continuing effects of the security dilemma; and perpetuation of the balance of power as a central feature of the system, both at global and regional levels.

Balance of power analysis inevitably involves assessing a constantly changing situation as membership of alliances and acquisition of military, economic, and scientific and technological capabilities constantly changes. However, it is certainly still the case that there are important global balances between Russia and its allies and the United States and its allies, and between China and the United States and its allies. At the regional level there are key balances between China and Japan, China and India, India and Pakistan, and between Israel and the leading states of the Muslim world (Egypt, Iran, Pakistan, and Saudi Arabia).

An inevitable corollary of an international system of states which is inherently anarchic, with no single power capable of controlling the world in a kind of global empire, is that states will experience the *security dilemma* and by reacting to it will perpetuate insecurity and conflict. In inter-state relations, a security dilemma will occur when states pursuing policies to enhance their own security (for example, by rearmament programmes or by forming alliances) unintentionally create feelings of increased insecurity. This leads to a vicious circle, security–insecurity, when states that feel increasingly vulnerable and insecure then decide to invest in enhancing their own security, in turn provoking a reaction by their perceived rival, leading to the enhancement of their new security.

The security dilemma provides at least a partial explanation of *arms races*. The most original thinking about the security dilemma in the international relations literature is to be found in Robert Jervis's *Perceptions and Misperceptions in International Politics* (1976), where he uses game theory to show that, if war is costly and cooperation is beneficial, there will be a possibility of breaking out of the security dilemma: if it can be shown that war is very expensive and risky, policies designed to reduce rather than increase inter-state tension and overcome mistrust and fear may be adopted. The concept of the security dilemma can usefully be applied to relations with non-state actors and this will be discussed in Chapter 2.

In the light of these perennial features of our international state system, the UK Foreign Secretary and his colleagues would be well advised to support a policy of sustaining a support of sufficient armaments and armed forces to defend the realm against any potential aggressor, even if there is no actual aggressor currently engaged in threatening UK security. The US government spends huge sums on defence, but even they are suffering from severe overstretch in terms of personnel and finance due to the huge costs of the Iraq War and occupation.

This is most certainly the defence policy that any wise government will be encouraged to adopt when it seeks advice from the chiefs of the armed services. This is the major lesson to be drawn by the UK foreign-policy makers from the experiences of both the Second World War and the cold war. Pacifism would have been useless in the face of the threat from Hitler in the Second World War and in response to Stalin's bid to expand the borders of his Soviet Communist Empire across Europe after Hitler's defeat.

It is salutary to remember that the Allies were only able to win the Second World War by the skin of their teeth, and the UK could not have done it without the help of the US. Similarly with the cold war: without the support of the US allies with their impressive ability to project their military powers and their lead in atomic weapons technology, large areas of Europe might well have suffered the same fate as Czechoslovakia and East Germany, Poland, Hungary, and the other countries of Eastern and Central Europe. They would have been swallowed up by the Russian bear.

The wisest rule of statecraft was stated by Vegetius writing in the 4th century AD. He wrote: *Qui desiderat pacem, praeparet bellum* (Let him who desires peace, prepare for war).

As we shall observe in the following section, the mere possession of large quantities of weapons and large numbers of troops does not necessarily mean that such a well protected state will become an aggressor. Much will depend on the statesmanship shown by a state's leaders and on the way they respond to the pressure of events. And while it is true that dictatorships and tyrannical one-party regimes have by their nature a greater propensity for coercive violence, especially against their own citizens, it is not necessarily the case that democracies distinguish themselves by their absence of coercive violent behaviour. Indeed, as we shall see in the following section, the powerful democracies have a track record of considerable coercive intervention in their foreign and security policies in recent years. Democracies do have a well deserved reputation for avoiding the use of force against fellow democracies. On the other hand, they have a track record of frequent military interventions in third states, often employing massive firepower and causing huge 'collateral damage', that is, death and destruction to civilian populations.

Coercive and liberal states

Coercion is the use or threat of physical force to compel, persuade or restrain. All states are inherently coercive because all government and regimes need to use force to enforce the law, to maintain internal order, and to defend the state against any perceived external threats. The only movement which is opposed in principle to the powers of government and the state's use of legal systems, implicitly backed by coercive power, is anarchism.

A survey of current political systems in the modern world shows that there are huge differences in the degree of coerciveness employed by states. At one end of the spectrum are states characterized by strong elements of liberalism and democracy where legislatures and governments are chosen by the people in free elections, governments and legislatures are accountable to the citizens and where basic human rights and liberties are upheld and the rule of law is maintained under an independent judiciary. In these liberal democratic states the coercive capabilities of the government and its security forces are not, in normal times, an intimidating and ever-present aspect of daily life on the streets. The police are trained to use minimum force and the military are generally deployed mainly for external defence rather than for internal coercion. Although the War on Terror waged since 9/11 has led many democracies to introduce stronger anti-terrorist measures, in no case has this led to the overturning of democratic institutions and the abandonment of liberal values.

Orwell's *1984* is an invaluable morality story for our times but in reality the citizens in liberal democracies still enjoy a huge amount of personal freedom. This is not to say that all liberal democracies have impeccable records in upholding liberal democratic values and in keeping their coercive powers under effective constraints with totally reliable procedures of scrutiny and accountability. There have been numerous instances of the abuse of coercive powers. Acton's famous dictum, 'all power corrupts and absolute power corrupts absolutely', is as true today as it was when he coined it. Even the world's greatest democracy, the United States of America, has a record of serious abuses of the coercive powers of the state, especially in the conduct of its foreign policy.

For example, in the late 20th century the US was involved in propping up numerous unsavoury dictatorships in Latin

America, not only turning a blind eye to the large-scale human rights violations by these regimes, but in many cases rendering them substantial financial, logistic, and military assistance in perpetuating their abuses of human rights. More recently there have been instances of clear abuse of international human rights standards, for example, the long-term detention without trial of prisoners alleged to have been involved in crimes of terrorism, abuse of prisoners at Abu Ghraib, and the rendition of suspects for questioning to regimes where torture is habitually practised.

On the other hand, we need to bear in mind that the US has been a major champion of the democratization process and the strengthening of human rights protection in many countries. During the cold war, US leadership of the democratic countries in defence of their values and institutions liberated millions from the misery of life under one-party Communist rule.

By far the worst abuses of coercive power in modern history were committed by totalitarian regimes of the 20th century: Hitler's Nazi regime which was responsible for the Holocaust and which occupied most of Europe in the 1940s; Stalin's Communist dictatorship which imposed on the Former Soviet Union, and the Warsaw Pact countries of Eastern Europe, one of the most repressive systems of totalitarian rule ever known; the Communist regime in China; and Pol Pot's regime in Cambodia. Millions died under these brutal regimes. They belong at the extreme opposite end of the spectrum of state coerciveness in the modern era from the liberal democracies described above.

However, there are some important caveats to bear in mind when one is constructing a typology of states based on the degree of coercion employed. First, there will be huge fluctuations in the amount of internal coercion used in the context of coercive changes in the type of regime. For example, there were extremely high levels of coercion involved in Nigeria during the period

> **Spectrum of state coerciveness**
>
> **Least coercive**
>
> **Operative liberal democracies** (e.g. the US and EU states)
>
> **Moderately coercive**
>
> **Traditional autocracies** (e.g. Saudi Arabia, Jordan, Morocco)
>
> **Highly coercive**
>
> **Dictatorships with some countervailing checks on power** (e.g. Mugabe's regime, Castro regime)
>
> **Most coercive**
>
> **Personal tyrannies** (e.g. Saddam Hussein in Iraq)
>
> **Totalitarian one party states** (e.g. Former Soviet Union, Nazi Germany, Pol Pot's regime)

when the secessionist state of Biafra was briefly established, but once this crisis was ended the level of coercion fell dramatically. The ceasefire and initial peace process in Sri Lanka, which it was hoped would bring a permanent end to conflict between the Tamil Tigers and the Sri Lankan government, provides another example of dramatic decline in coerciveness. The reverse trend, i.e. a dramatic increase in coerciveness, has occurred in Nepal where the previously peaceful kingdom has been confronted by a Maoist guerrilla insurgency. Second, there are, as one would expect, huge fluctuations in coerciveness of states which embark on, or become involved in, full-scale war. For example, Operation Shock and Awe, which was employed by the United States and United Kingdom when they invaded Iraq in 2003, was one of the most dramatic examples of the use of massive firepower, a deliberate use of coercive military force to commence a war which did not have a mandate of approval from the United Nations Security

Council. Hence, although the US and the UK fall into the category of democracies least reliant on the use or threat of coercive power for their internal governance, both countries have been involved in extreme coerciveness as an instrument of foreign policy.

Economic coercion

It is a mistake to view the use of military or police powers as the only form of coercion open to the state. In domestic policies the state may embark on draconian economic measures, for example, Mugabe's expropriation of the lands of white farmers, Stalin's 'collectivization' of agriculture in the 1930s, and the rather ruthless exploitation of state control over the economy in countries such as North Korea and Belarus. There has been a debate in the neo-Marxist literature about the theory of so-called 'structural violence' as a form of coercion within the capitalist democracies. It is pointed out that what is often described as 'free bargaining', for example, between the worker and the employer, is in effect no such thing because the power of the parties to the bargaining process is so unequal. A poor man who may be the sole provider for his family who becomes unemployed in a time of recession may have no realistic alternative but to take a poorly paid job with poor working conditions in order to support his family. This is certainly not 'free bargaining', but nor is it coercion by the state. It should be more accurately described as economic exploitation by the employer. Moreover, we should take into account that most democracies have adopted social welfare policies which at least mitigate the effects of unemployment and low income on the poorest members of society (for example, forms of national insurance, health care, free education, income support, and other forms of welfare benefits). I am therefore excluding the so-called 'structural violence' in capitalist societies from the coercive powers used by the state.

However, there are innumerable instances of states using coercive economic measures in the form of sanctions as instruments of foreign policy. Such measures are deliberately aimed at coercing the targeted state to change its policies, and recent history shows that, although they have a mixed track record, they can sometimes be effective. The UK's attempts to bring pressure on the Southern Rhodesian regime when it declared independence in 1965 were ineffective because Ian Smith's government was able to secure supplies of vital material, such as oil, via South Africa. However, economic sanctions against the Apartheid regime in South Africa did make a major contribution to persuading the Nationalist Party government to negotiate an end to Apartheid because the international economic pressure, significantly including the United States, was having a major impact on the South African business community. Another striking example of the power of economic sanctions as a coercive measure to cause major reorientation of a state's policy was the case of Libya. It is widely agreed that the economic measures adopted by the US and the international community in 1991 in connection with two Libyans indicted on charges of involvement in the Pan Am 103 sabotage bombing over Lockerbie, Scotland, in December 1988, played a key part in persuading Colonel Gaddafi to hand over the two suspects for trial by Scottish judges held in Holland. The measures that really put pressure on the Gaddafi regime included a prohibition on the export to Libya of vital items of energy industry technology needed by Libya for the exploitation of their gas and oil reserves, and restrictions on trade which prevented Libya from expanding its trade with the EU countries and the US at a time when the regime was desperate to deepen its economic links with Western countries and to attract Western capital investment. The prohibition of direct flights to Libya was far less significant in economic terms but it was humiliating for the Gaddafi regime. Carefully selected and targeted economic sanctions can coerce specific regimes in certain circumstances, especially when the measures are widely supported and implemented by the international community.

The epitome of the coercive state

What are the major features of the coercive state? It is not surprising to find that they are wholly incompatible with the key characteristics of liberal democratic states. Whereas the latter come to power by the consent of the governed, that is through regularly conducted free elections, the typical coercive regime achieves power as a result of a *coup*, a revolution, or a successful insurgency, often supported only by a small minority of the population, and frequently resorting to terror attacks against civilians as part of its tactics for seizing power. Once in power the typical coercive state almost instinctively employs extreme violence or terror to intimidate and suppress any threat to its power or even on the pretext of threats or dissent which are shown to be imagined rather than real.

Once in control of the state machine, the military, and the police, the typical coercive state tends to arrogate all power to itself and to use any available means to maintain its monopoly. In other words, they exercise power with total ruthlessness with the full endorsement of the dictatorship. Although they always seek to appropriate the language of legitimacy and legality they have no concept of the rule of law as it is known in an operative liberal democracy. There is no set of constitutional impediments or checks and balances which can constrain them because they see themselves as above the law. The law is whatever they decree it to be at any given moment. There is no independent judiciary: those who dispense the dictatorship's 'laws' are creatures of the dictatorship and their so-called courts are a mockery of justice. Extra-judicial murders, torture, mass deportation, and even massacres are carried out at the behest of the dictatorship which actually orders these crimes.

Political opponents who are seen as potentially dangerous will be either killed or incarcerated in solitary confinement. The typical security agency of the coercive state is the secret police, and spying on the population, surveillance, and harassment are constant activities, along with attempts to control the media and to censor anything to which the dictatorship takes exception. The typical coercive state will also seek to ensure that all the other organs of social organization and communication, for example, places of worship, educational institutions, trade unions, and professional organizations are constantly monitored to ensure that they do not become channels for mobilizing dissent and opposition to the regime. However, the attempt by dictatorships to control the flow of information and ideas has become far more difficult as a result of globalization and the development of the internet and other media technologies. Ultimately it is this inability to control the flow of information and ideas across international borders that has made the entire project of constructing a new totalitarian dictatorship far less feasible today than it was in the 1950s and 1960s. Personal tyrannies and one-party states still exist but the above analysis suggests that they are more vulnerable than ever today to revolutions from below. In many ways the velvet revolutions at the end of the cold war were the precursors. The appetite for democracy and freedom is contagious. Events in Iraq, the Ukraine, and Lebanon in 2005 are encouraging evidence of this trend, although in Iraq, at the time of writing, the efforts to construct a new democratic constitution acceptable to the Sunni population as well as the Shia and Kurds are encountering considerable difficulties.

Finally, we should note that the typical coercive state of the early 21st century is not a one-party regime. It is a ruling party dominated regime. Frequently a number of tame political parties in addition to the ruling party are tolerated on the strict understanding that they must never threaten the controlling position of the dictatorship's own party. If a token dissenting party steps out of line and becomes a serious nuisance to the regime it will be suppressed ruthlessly.

3. Ayatollah Khomeini (1900–89) led the Iranian revolution which overthrew the Shah (1979). He was leader of Iran during its war with Iraq (1980–8) and the US hostage crisis.

The typical dictatorship takes a similar line on religious faiths or movements. Provided a religious organization keeps out of politics and avoids any criticism of the dictatorship's policies and actions it will generally be permitted to continue to conduct religious services. However, even this limited degree of religious toleration can hold hidden dangers for the dictatorship. For example, in Poland under Communist rule it was not only the courage of Solidarity trade union leader Lech Walesa and his colleagues who provided leadership of the resistance to the Communist dictatorship. The Catholic Church, traditionally a major influence in Polish life, provided an important alternative value-system and intellectual framework to the dreary diet of Marxist-Leninist ideology pumped out by the Communist leaders. Religion can function as a powerful catalyst for opposition and potentially, for outright defiance and resistance to the regime.

This can apply just as much to the Muslim religion. For example, it was Ayatollah Khomeini and his supporters who became the catalyst for the fundamentalist Iranian revolution which mobilized mass support in the streets and toppled the Shah's regime. Ironically, no sooner had they disposed of Riza Shah Pahlavi then they proceeded to establish a religious fundamentalist dictatorship far more repressive in character and which used terror against its designated 'enemies' both internal and external. Religiously motivated revolutions or rebellions do not inevitably lead to democratic forms of government being established. The fate of Afghanistan following the seizure of power by the Taliban is a clear example of a religiously motivated extremist regime gaining power and introducing a ferociously repressive regime, in many respects a throwback to the Dark Ages.

The debate on totalitarianism

The most influential work in the concept and theory of totalitarianism is Hannah Arendt's *The Origins of Totalitarianism*

(1958). Her conception of totalitarianism is founded on the theory of a mass society in which traditional ties and intermediate organizations and loyalties have been destroyed by the devastating effects of war. In these conditions, Arendt posits, the isolated individual is vulnerable to being mobilized to a new loyalty, a bond of total loyalty and subservience to a charismatic leader, such as Hitler, who by manipulating the masses can construct a system of centralized control which rules and subdues its opponents by means of state terror on a massive scale. In my view, this remains the most persuasive and powerful theory of the origins of totalitarianism. In an influential study, which was originally published five years after Arendt's, Carl Friedrich and Zbigniew Brzezinski identify the following key characteristics of a totalitarian system: (i) A totalitarian ideology professing to be universal in its applicability and a 'true' theory to govern the life of the individual and the state; (ii) a single mass party under the leadership of the dictatorship; (iii) a system of state terror in which the key instrument is the secret police; (iv) total control over communications; (v) a monopoly of control of the military and military armaments; and (vi) centralized control over the economy. The major point of difference between Friedrich and Brzezinski and Arendt is that the latter does not view a totalitarian universalist ideology as an essential component of a totalitarian system of rule, and she places greater emphasis on the role of absolute terror as an instrument of the totalitarian regime.

However, it is implicit in Friedrich and Brzezinski's concept that a truly totalitarian regime is only feasible in a relatively developed country with a high degree of industrialization, and modern communications and technology. It could be argued that, in the light of more recent developments in technology such as the internet, the degree of control over communications and the flow of information implied in the Friedrich and Brzezinski model is no longer practicable. New technologies have become a powerful weapon for challenging state power.

Rosemary O'Kane, one of the most perceptive comparative analysts of the coercive state, points to another serious problem with the classic theories of totalitarianism described above. In her analysis of the case of Cambodia in the zero years she shows that the Pol Pot regime, which massacred hundreds of thousands of Cambodians in the mid-1970s, did not have access to the modern technology and communications implicit in Friedrich and Brzezinski's model of totalitarianism, or a modern bureaucracy. Cambodia was an underdeveloped largely agrarian country. Nor did the Pol Pot regime have a complex universalist ideology. Instead the regime concentrated on inculcating socio-economic resentment among the peasants and used this, combined with a populist form of nationalism, to turn the rural dwellers against the city dwellers, and particularly against the small middle class and the intellectuals. However, as O'Kane concludes, there are features of the Pol Pot regime which bear a close resemblance to the Arendt model: Cambodia had been devastated by warfare; traditional ties and intermediate organizations at local level were severely disrupted or destroyed (and the regime's enforced movement of hundreds of thousands of the population exacerbated the level of socio-economic crisis); and, above all, the regime fully demonstrated its capacity for absolute terror by mass killing on a genocidal scale, albeit using its guerrilla army rather than a secret police to implement the terror.

Rosemary O'Kane makes the valuable proposal that the more accurate way to describe the Pol Pot regime is as a *rudimentary totalitarianism*, which has its origins in 'the uprooting of societies through the decimation of foreign and civil war'. In other words, it may be a serious error to assume that the totalitarian model of the coercive state applies exclusively to developed, industrialized societies. The severe effects of conflict, destruction, and the uprooting of societies which can be witnessed in so many war-torn regions of the world could well have the effect of stimulating growth of fresh proto-totalitarian and rudimentary totalitarian regimes.

4. The skulls are those of victims of Pol Pot's policy of mass murder in Cambodia in the 1970s, which led to the deaths of an estimated two million people.

Murderous personal tyrannies: Idi Amin and Saddam Hussein

Idi Amin's regime in Uganda began when he seized power from the government of President Milton Obote on 25 January, 1971, and lasted until a successful counter-*coup* by the Tanzanian armed forces and exiles of the Uganda Liberation Front succeeded in removing him in April 1979. The *coup* which brought Amin to power was relatively bloodless, causing less than 100 casualties, and was initially popular among the majority of Ugandans. Amin promised to get rid of the corruption and favouritism which he claimed characterized the Obote government. He pledged free elections, the release of political prisoners, and the scrapping of the martial law imposed by the Obote government. The reality was to be vastly different. Amin soon consolidated his power by taking control of the army, purged it of officers and soldiers who had been loyal supporters of the former regime, and filled it with

Amin loyalists, especially Palestinians and Sudanese troops. There was certainly nothing new about using the army as an instrument of control under dictatorship. What was different about Amin's regime was the cruelty and ruthlessness he used to consolidate and maintain his power.

Amin transformed his regime from a military dictatorship into a personal tyranny. In the process he killed an estimated 300,000 people, mainly members of tribes other than his own. Many were thrown into prison, tortured, and then killed on direct orders from Amin. His main instruments of state terror became the State Research Bureau, Public Safety Unit, and the army. In the autumn of 1972 Amin expelled the Ugandan Asian community to Britain, having made the absurd claim that they were undermining the Ugandan economy. In reality the small Ugandan Asian minority was potentially one of Uganda's main assets because of its business and professional skills.

One of the recurrent features of personal tyrannies in Africa and elsewhere is that the dictator often makes decisions that are wholly irrational, that is against their own longer term interests. This is all too evident in the case of the Mugabe regime in Zimbabwe, where the expropriation of the lands of the white farmers has virtually destroyed the rural economy. Ironically it was Amin's unbelievable incompetence in managing the Ugandan economy that was his undoing. In order to court popularity with Ugandans he decided to nationalize all the major foreign-owned businesses in the country. This had the effect of scaring away foreign investment, causing a serious drop in productivity, increasing inflation, and providing Amin and his henchmen with an ideal opportunity for increased personal enrichment through corruption and embezzlement. In the last two years of his rule the economy of Amin's Uganda totally collapsed.

A depressing asset of the Amin regime in Uganda, which again has been a recurrent theme in other dictatorships in Africa and elsewhere in the developing world, was the initial willingness of the United Kingdom and other countries to turn a blind eye to Amin's major human rights violations and to sell him large quantities of weapons. However, after 1973 when Amin began to form closer relations with the Soviet Union, and in the wake of the 1976 Entebbe hijack, when Amin was shown to be hand in glove with the terrorists, relations with the West sharply declined.

Amin finally overreached himself in April 1979, when he foolishly decided to invade Tanzania. In response Tanzanian troops invaded Uganda. Large numbers of Amin's forces either deserted or surrendered, Amin suffered a humiliating defeat and was swept from power.

Amin's regime is a very clear example of a personal tyranny. It appears to have had no recognizable ideology and this made it very easy for Amin to switch sides and curry favour with the Soviet Union after initially seeking weapons, supplies, and other resources from the West. A common feature of personal tyrannies is that their lack of any basic ideological foundation enables them to be entirely promiscuous and exploitative in their relations with foreign powers.

The personal tyranny of Saddam Hussein over Iraq, 1979–2003, inflicted enormous suffering on the Iraqi Kurdish population and on the Shi'ite population, and also on the Marsh Arabs. There is of course ample historical evidence that dictatorships which are threatened by, or perceive they are in danger of the break-up of their territory as a result of ethno-nationalist insurgency tend to use the most brutal and extreme forms of coercion to suppress the insurgency. The recent history of Burma, Indonesia, Congo-Zaire, Sudan, and many other states exemplifies this trend very clearly. However, even by the standards of draconian repression of nationalist upsurge Saddam Hussein's record was exceptionally brutal.

Indeed, in the eyes of respected human rights organizations, such as Human Rights Watch, the violence and terror used by the Saddam regime against the Kurds was on near-genocidal scale. Kurdish nationalism has always been strong among the Iraqi Kurds and the *peshmerga*, their guerrilla fighters, constantly harassed the Iraqi regime in the years before Saddam took power. During the Iran–Iraq War, 1980–8, the Kurdish nationalists saw their opportunity to take control over what they regarded as their territory in northern Iraq. The various Kurdish factors united under the umbrella of the Iraqi Kurdistan Front. With some help and encouragement from the Iranians they proceeded to mount a very effective campaign against Saddam's army. In response Saddam decided to inflict a terrible vengeance on the Kurds.

Thousands of Kurdish villages were destroyed and mass deportations and massacres of Kurds were carried out. In March 1988 Saddam's forces resorted to the use of chemical weapons against the civilians in the town of Halabja, causing the death of over 6,000. The precise number of those killed in Saddam's brutal attempt to suppress the Iraqi Kurds will never be known, but it is certainly over 100,000.

In the wake of the first Gulf War to liberate Kuwait from Iraqi occupation the Kurds again went on the offensive against Saddam's regime and reoccupied their land in northern Iraq. However, the US and UK governments were not ready or willing to intervene and support the Kurds' bid for autonomy, and Saddam once again mounted a ruthless campaign to regain control over northern Iraq. Faced with the terrible plight of hundreds of thousands of Kurdish refugees fleeing through snow-covered mountains to Turkey, and many more into Iran, the Western Coalition which had liberated Kuwait declared that they would guarantee the Kurds safe haven in the Kurdish area of northern Iraq, send in humanitarian relief, and attempt to ensure protection of the Kurds by the use of patrols by Allied military aircraft. Since the toppling of the Saddam regime in 2003 the Kurds have been able to enjoy relative security. They took a full part in the first free elections in Iraq in January 2005 and in the talks on a new federal constitution for Iraq.

There are two main lessons to be drawn from the epic of Saddam's attempts to suppress the Kurds. First, if the coercive state is prepared to deploy its superior firepower without any political or humanitarian restraint, and there is no intervention from a more powerful state or coalition of states to protect a minority targeted with extreme repression and terror, the coercive state can succeed, at least temporarily, in suppressing the physical capability of the insurgents to resist.

However, the second key lesson from the epic struggle of the Kurds against Saddam's personalized tyranny is that there are severe limits to what absolute terror and brutal coercion can achieve. In Milton's memorable worlds, 'Who overcomes by force, hath overcome but half his foe' (*Paradise Lost*, 1. 648).

A determined minority, particularly one with a powerful aspiration for autonomy or self-determination, can still present a latent potential threat even after decades of brutal repression, because they have the motivation and belief in their cause to sustain a spirit of resistance even in their darkest hours.

The proper use of force in the liberal state

There is a crucial difference between the use of illegitimate coercion, or violence, by a state that ignores the norms of the rule of law in domestic and international policy and the proper use of legitimate force under the constitutional and legal checks and balances of the liberal state. There are clearly many circumstances when the use of force is not only justifiable but positively obligatory if the rule of law, national security, and public safety are to be upheld.

Citizens have a duty, for example, to assist the state in defence of the community against external attack. And there are clear obligations to defend and uphold the constitution and enforce the laws. It has been observed earlier in this discussion that there also may be circumstances in which the citizens may have a moral obligation to use force unilaterally against leaders or state officials who have seriously derogated from, subverted, or overturned the liberal democratic constitution. The problem of the right use of force, however, raises not only issues of moral legitimacy and legality but also some difficult questions concerning the way in which forces should be employed. Who should be entrusted with the execution of force? How much force should be used?

In the case of external attack the normal agency of the state responsible for defence is the armed forces, and in a democracy both government and citizens will expect these defence forces to use whatever force is required to repel attack and defeat the enemy. Moreover it is a cardinal and long-standing principle of democratic government that the armed services should be firmly under ultimate civil control by the democratically responsible government. But responsibility for tasks of internal security has been a matter of serious contention in many liberal states. Should the civil police take on the job as a natural extension of their police law-enforcement function? Should responsibility be shared by police and army, the latter being called in to tackle the more serious outbreaks of political violence and unrest? Or should there be a 'third force', on the model of the French CRS, specially designated, trained, and equipped to tackle domestic political violence? The precise formula adopted has tended to vary widely in accordance with constitutional and juridical tradition. Clear advantage may be gained from a tradition of unarmed police using low-profile and gentle methods and maintaining public support and sympathetic cooperation. These benefits must, however, be weighed against the concomitant lack of decisive physical presence and firepower necessary to defeat armed insurgents.

In all liberal democracies the army is regarded as the last line of defence against internal disorders, and various constitutional and legal formulas exist to invoke their aid to the civil power in severe disturbances and emergencies. However, whatever the balance of forces deployed by the state to deal with internal violence, there are certain basic principles which must govern the use of such force by the liberal state.

First and foremost, security agencies must operate entirely within the framework of law. If they defy the rule of law under the pretence of protecting it they undermine the integrity, authority, and public respect for the law which is essential to the continuance of constitutional democracy. Some individual sections and members of police and security forces will be tempted to accrete extra-legal powers and to hide behind the shield of 'superior orders' and 'security interests'. Others may unwittingly be misled, in the absence of clearly defined legal responsibilities and procedures, into taking actions which expose them to civil actions and public prosecutions. The most evil and dangerous consequence that may follow from repeated overturning of the rule of law is the establishment of a power-hungry security apparatus which acquires an appetite for extra-judicial reprisal. Alas Solzhenitsyn was too sanguine in assuming that 'the only punitive organ in human history that combined in one set of hands investigation, arrest, interrogation, prosecution, trial and execution of the verdict' was the Cheka. Democracies have no magical immunity against such cancerous growths, and their citizens and political leaders have a duty to ensure that police and security services operate within the constitution and the law. It is noteworthy that the Congressional Church Committee investigation into the US Secret Services' activities, while admitting the difficult problems entailed in firm political control and surveillance of such operations, repeatedly spells out the importance of this lesson for the health of the US political system.

The clear corollary of operating within the rule of law is the maintenance of absolutely clear and firm democratic control over police and security services and operations. Some modern counter-insurgency specialists constantly reiterate their demand for these services to be kept under a single unified control. Although a case may be made for this on the grounds of economy of resources, secrecy, and effectiveness, we should also recognize the dangers inherent in such a unified structure. There are obvious traditional weaknesses of administrative centralization such as bureaucratic remoteness, insensitivity, and cumbersome decision-making procedures. Additional dangers may stem from 'monopolistic' security organizations abusing their power, losing their identification with local communities, and forfeiting invaluable popular trust and support.

The other major principle governing the right use of force by the liberal state is the doctrine of minimal force. This principle has been the predominant guide to the British police forces in the matter of political violence throughout their history. In essence it has meant the use of minimum force to deter, restrain, or, if necessary, contain violence, and to preserve public order. To exercise the police function with such restraint inevitably calls for superb discipline and professionalism, a studied impartiality and neutrality in matters of political controversy, and considerable patience and moral courage.

Minimal force does not simply apply to crowd control and potentially violent or disruptive demonstrations and processions. The essential principle can also be applied to armed response and armed violence. In such circumstances the aims of minimal force must be to protect the public, to bring about the rapid disarming and peaceful surrender of the armed persons involved, and to bring them before the courts on criminal charges. Contrast the purely military aim in time of war of identifying the enemy and shooting them on sight. One of the reasons why soldiers find it so onerous and unnatural to take on a constabulary minimal-force role is that it is essentially alien to their military training and ethos.

But can minimal force really work effectively when the security forces face a sizeable number of heavily armed and ruthless insurgents? Historical experience indicates that liberal states need to react much more positively and forcefully to defeat armed revolutionaries, guerrillas, and terrorists. In what is, after all, an internal war situation, the forces of the state have to be empowered to take war measures, to go on the offensive and to use all military means necessary to defeat a direct challenge to the survival of the state. I would argue that the doctrine of minimal force is only really effective in circumstances where there is a relatively high degree of political consensus and social cohesion, cooperation, and discipline. It fails to work where large sections of the population deny the legitimacy of the state, and where many view the police and army as alien, hostile, and oppressive.

In sum, I am arguing that, while the doctrine of minimal force is a sensible and comfortably reassuring one for a democracy, we should be constantly critically re-examining our level of force in the light of changing threats and potential for violence in international relations. While democracies should avoid over-reliance on military force they do need adequate means of self-defence.

There is another reason why we should be conscious of the limitations of minimal force doctrine. We must avoid falling into the habit of believing that the possession of adequate force for legal sanctions and defence is sufficient unto the day, a panacea for all forms of social and political violence. Force may restrain or punish or defend but it cannot reconcile and heal.

Positive political cooperation and unification require the building of allegiances, loyalties, trust and confidence, and greater mutual understanding. Force cannot bring these things about, though certainly a restrained and humane use of force is less likely to destroy positive political cooperation than unrestrained and overwhelming force. But the necessary vehicles for bringing about positive political progress must be effective communication, dialogue, and mutual education. To restore a parched and stricken political community one needs to irrigate it by replenishing or creating afresh the vital channels of political culture.

Weak, failed, and quasi-states

In briefing the new Secretary of State, the senior adviser is unlikely to spend long on very weak and failed states, unless a crisis involving a state of this kind and the United States is seen to have a particular interest or responsibility. The Secretary of State will probably never see files of papers regarding, for example, the tiny microstates of Oceania, the Pacific Islands of Melanesia, Polynesia, and Micronesia. However, it would be a mistake to equate small size with acute economic deprivation. For example, in 2000, French Polynesia's 200,000 population enjoyed a GDP (Gross Domestic Product) per head of $28,000 US dollars, and a higher total GDP than Papua New Guinea with a population of almost five million. Iceland, with a population of 300,000 has a total GDP of almost $8 billion dollars and a higher GDP per head than Belgium; and Andorra, one of the world's tiniest states, with a population of 100,000 has an estimated GDP of over $1 billion dollars. So long as these tiny states remain financially viable and continue to meet their international obligations and abide by the rules of international trade and diplomacy, they are unlikely to figure in the new Secretary of State's daily briefings.

The Secretary of State will need to be briefed very fully on what some political scientists have called *failed states* because they are, by definition, already experiencing profound political crisis, in some cases civil strife and acute economic crises and instabilities. Many of the countries that fall into this category are in Africa where in all cases political and economic crises have been deepened by the tragic HIV/Aids epidemic. For example, Congo-Brazzaville, Zimbabwe, and Eritrea are among the ten countries in the world with the highest number of AIDS cases per 100,000 of the population.

A further tragic irony is that Eritrea spends the highest percentage of GDP on defence of any country, and Congo-Brazzaville is twelfth in the same defence spending league table.

The states to which the new Secretary of State will be required to give the most urgent attention are those in a state of serious crisis and where the US has committed US troops, now almost invariably in alliance with other NATO partners, in an effort to provide the necessary basic security to facilitate longer term economic recovery and political stability. In 2005–6 the two thickest files falling into this category would be those covering Iraq and Afghanistan.

Despite the popularity of the term 'failed states' one could argue that it has questionable value in the contemporary international system. One of the most significant features of contemporary international relations is that even the weakest and most crisis-ridden states are protected by the now well established norms of the post-colonial era. In the heyday of colonization such countries would have been immediate targets for imperial conquest and exploitation by more powerful states in the international system. Today, states are expected to adhere to the norms of anti-colonialism and to uphold the right of all the former colonized countries to self-determination and sovereign independence on the basis of equal status with all other states in the international system. Effectively this means that once a state has become part of our international system it automatically retains its status as an independent sovereign country even when it is woefully misgoverned by its rulers, and even when it is experiencing civil war and other large-scale internal violence and economic crisis. The United Nations Charter does provide for action under Chapter VII which may include military intervention in certain emergency situations which are deemed by the UN Security Council to be a threat to international peace and security.

Although the unilateral decision of the US and UK governments to invade Iraq in the absence of a specific UN resolution authorizing such action defied this international norm against unilateral military intervention, there is no clear evidence that this persuaded the rest of the international community to abandon the norm of non-intervention.

So what term should we use to describe those states which are experiencing internal violence on a massive, in some cases genocidal, scale and which appear to be in a situation of complete internal chaos and crisis, but which still have the formal status of states, recognized by other states, rights of representation at the UN and other international fora? I would suggest that the term *quasi-states* is a more appropriate designation for these states which enjoy the status and symbols of independent statehood but which patently lack the political will and basic capacity for effective governance required to deliver the basic socio-economic needs and security required by their citizens.

The role of the individual and the state

One way of examining international relations is through the role of unique individuals. As E. H. Carr argued in *What is History?*, the study of the idiographic (i.e. individuals) is just as valid and necessary as the study of broad trends and patterns in human societies if we are to gain a fuller understanding of history. Exactly the same argument applies to the study of international relations.

5. Prince Otto von Bismarck (1815–98) was Prime Minister of Prussia (1862–90). He used Prussia's military strength and his political cunning to defeat Austria and France and become the first Chancellor of the German Reich in 1871.

For example, how could one adequately explain the emergence of French hegemony in 17th-century Europe without taking into account the clever statecraft of Cardinal de Richelieu (1585–1642) who became Chief Minister to Louis XIII of France? Richelieu's masterstroke was to align France with the Protestant powers in the Thirty Years War, thus greatly enhancing French power at the expense of France's major rival, Spain. How could one explain the breakdown of the 18th-century balance of power in Europe without reference to the career of Napoleon Bonaparte, who for a limited period succeeded in dominating a large part of Europe? And how can one understand the way in which Napoleon's bid for domination was defeated and how a new balance of power was created at the Congress of Vienna without examining the role of British statesman, Viscount Castlereagh, who, as British Foreign Secretary (1812–22) led the Grand Alliance against Napoleon and, with Prince Klemens von Metternich the Austrian Foreign Minister and Chancellor, created the new Concert of Powers which succeeded in maintaining a general peace in Europe for over half a century? And what chance would the student of international politics in Europe have of understanding the developments which ultimately undermined the European balance of power in the 19th century without a proper consideration of the policies of Prince Otto von Bismarck, Prime Minister of Prussia (1862–90), who masterminded the defeat of France and Austria and brought about the unification of Germany?

Nor is the key role of individual statesmen and leaders restricted to the autocracies and traditional monarchies of the pre-democratic era. It is hard to underestimate the contribution of Georges 'Tiger' Clemenceau, Premier of France 1917–20, to Allied victory in the First World War and to the shaping of the Treaty of Versailles. Similarly, it would be impossible to explain the determined and ultimately successful British struggle to defeat Hitler without taking into account the key role of Winston Churchill as wartime Prime Minister. How very different things would have been if Neville Chamberlain had somehow survived in

Karikatur auf den Wiener Kongreß.   Zeitgenössisches Flugblatt.

6. The Congress of Vienna (1814–15), where European statesmen attempted to solve the European territorial problems resulting from the Napoleonic Wars.

office or if the premiership had fallen into the hands of a politician who still clung to the policy of appeasement towards Germany.

It is easy to find examples of dictators in recent history who had a colossal impact on the shape of international relations: Adolf Hitler, Joseph Stalin, and Mao Tse-Tung are obvious examples. And in attempting to explain the ending of the cold war and the implosion of the Soviet Union, it would be absurd to overlook the major role of Mikhail Gorbachev, General Secretary of the Soviet Communist Party 1988–91. Gorbachev's personal commitment to developing communism with a human face and ending the confrontation with the West were of seminal importance. His political reforms ended the Communist Party's monopoly of power and paved the way for a break-up of the Soviet Union.

Last but not least we should not neglect the huge importance of the common man, particularly important in times of major crises

7. **Trench warfare, where armies confronted each other in trenches, notably in the 1914–18 war, led to slaughter on a massive scale. Allied victory was won at a huge cost in soldier's lives.**

and war. The sacrifices of millions of individuals made possible our enjoyment of freedom in the democracies of today. It was that wisest of all liberal political philosophers, John Stuart Mill, who observed: 'The worth of a state, in the long run is the worth of the individuals composing it'.

It is again all too easy to overlook the importance of the character and qualities of a state's citizens when attempting to assess the state's power and influence. The dramatist Jean Giraudoux, in his play *Tiger at the Gates* about the war between the Greeks and the Trojans, makes Ulysses muse aloud about the strength of nations:

A nation doesn't put itself at odds with its destiny by its crimes, but by its faults. Its army may be strong, its treasury well filled, its poets at the height if inspiration. But one day, why no one knows, because of some simple event … the nation is suddenly lost.

Total disappearance of a nation-state would indeed be a rare event in today's world. Indeed the durability of the state as the fundamental unit of the international system is one of the basic realities for any student of international relations. Nevertheless there are international relations scholars who argue that the state is becoming obsolete because even reasonably well-resourced states are unable to deal with the serious challenges posed by transnational phenomena such as climate change, major natural disaster, international organized crime, pandemics such as AIDS, and so on, and because greater regional economic integration and major reform of the UN may now be, according to their view, more promising as a framework for assisting very weak states.

As we have observed there is a huge variety of states. Many are so weak that they can best be viewed as quasi or failing states. Some are extremely unpleasant and dangerous not only to their citizens but to the wider international community. Despite this there is no sign of citizens wishing to abandon their state structures in favour of some integrated system of global or even regional governance. The recent rejection of the EU's draft Constitution by the voters in key member states suggests that even in the EU, a region of the world with long experience of substantial economic integration, there is no appetite for joining a superstate. Let us be realistic. The modern state is not seen as obsolescent by its citizens. With all its imperfections and problems the state seems to be here to stay.

Chapter 2
Non-states

Religions

It would be a great mistake to assume that people everywhere define their identity primarily in terms of the state in which they reside. For millions of people, especially those who live within the borders of multi-religious and multi-ethnic states, their primary identity will be defined by their religion, or by a mixture of their religion and their ethnicity. All the world's major religions originated before the emergence of the modern state. In our secular age, when many of us in Western countries take it for granted that there should be a clear separation between religious institutions and the state, it is quite often overlooked that religion has been the single most powerful influence not only on societal values, morality, and the norms and practices of family and community life: it has also had a major impact on the nature of the state itself, its laws and institutions and processes of government.

For example, Christianity was the major influence in the shaping of the European nation-state and the state system generally. The moral foundations of international law and the concept of international society are to be found in Christianity. This is most clearly seen in the masterwork of international law by Hugo Grotius (1583–1645), *De Jure Belli ac Pacis* (On the Law of

War and Peace) (1625). Grotius posits the key idea of a society of states sharing sufficient solidarity on the common principles that should govern inter-state relations, even in times of conflict, so that international law would not only be respected, it would be enforced. According to the rules of Grotian international law the rights of states to go to war are strictly limited and military force should only be used for the benefit of the whole international society. Sadly these principles remain idealistic aspirations: today one could hardly argue that Grotian ideas of the basic norms of international society and humanitarian restraints in the course of inter-state and internal warfare are respected and implemented by nation-states generally.

To sum up briefly, the impact of religious movements and institutions has been decidedly mixed. On the one hand, Christianity, Islam, and Judaism have all inspired humanitarian activities by both the rulers and the ruled, including the movement to abolish slavery, the International Red Cross movement, and Christian socialism aimed at ameliorating the conditions of the working classes. On the other, religions have motivated and inspired some of the most brutal inter-state and internal wars and terrorist campaigns. Yet the long-term influence of religion in helping to inspire and establish movements for the protection and enhancement of human rights for aid and development in the world's poorest countries has been a hugely positive contribution to the betterment of humanity.

However, we would be making a great mistake if we thought this was the only way in which religion can influence international relations. Religious institutions and movements have intervened directly in politics with quite dramatic effects. One example from recent history would be the way in which the Catholic Church acted as a focus of resistance to Communism. The ultimate success of the Solidarity movement in bringing Polish liberation from Communist rule owed a great deal to the determined support of both the Catholic Church in Poland and

8. Pope John Paul II (1920–2005), born in Poland, was the first non-Italian to be elected Pope since 1522, and is credited with helping to hasten the collapse of communism in Eastern Europe and generally.

the Polish-born Pope John Paul II. In Iran the overthrow of the Shah of Iran (1979) was led by Ayatollah Khomeini, the architect of the revolution which brought a militant Islamic fundamentalist regime to power and changed the balance of power in the Gulf and the wider Middle East. The former would be viewed by liberal-minded people as a good example of religion serving as a powerful ally in the struggle for political freedom and democracy, but the religious revolution in Iran, which put an authoritarian theocracy into power, can be seen as a regressive step both for the Iranian people and for the future of Iran's international relations.

This negative aspect of the influence of religion on international relations is of course by no means confined to the Islamic world. Jewish extremists in Israel, for example, have bitterly opposed any proposals for handing back lands in Gaza and the West Bank on the grounds that these are part of 'Biblical Israel' and must be defended at all costs. Note that it was a Jewish religious extremist who assassinated Prime Minister Yitzhak Rabin in 1995, thereby dealing a major blow to the Oslo peace accords.

Our new US Secretary of State should be briefed in considerable detail about the influence of religious extremists not only in the Middle East but worldwide. She should be advised to take a close interest in inter-faith dialogue, to be fully aware of the extent to which Islamist extremists are involved in the Al Qaeda network, the most dangerous form of international terrorism faced by the international community today. If this ruthless fanaticism is to be opposed effectively, the Secretary of State will need to work with her opposite numbers around the world to enlist moderate religious leaders everywhere to combine their efforts to dissuade angry alienated young Muslims from being recruited into the Al Qaeda or jihadi networks. Non-state religious movements, institutions, and leaders would not have been part of a Secretary of State's briefing during the cold war. Today it is as important that she knows about these as it is that she knows about the policies of major states, for these non-state networks pose a threat to the security not only of the US and its allies, but also to many medium and small states in the international community who may well have supposed that they were immune from such attacks. Why should Kenya and Tanzania, for example, have been chosen as venues for attacks on US embassies in August 1998? The attacks came like a bolt out of the blue, killing over 240, most of whom were citizens of Nairobi going about their daily business. I shall return to the challenge posted by terrorist groups in a later section, but first we must consider a second major category of non-state phenomena with an enduring and massive influence on international relations: nationalist movements.

Nationalism

Medieval Europe was innocent of modern doctrines of nationalism. Linked by the concept (if not by the reality) of a united Christendom and by the common language of the Catholic

Church, the states of medieval Europe constituted parcels of dynastic inheritance. The boundaries of these empires, kingdoms, and principalities were often ill-defended, and were drawn without regard for ethnic, linguistic, or religious homogeneity. The kingdom was what the king could hold against the military and diplomatic rivalry of his competitors and the king's subjects therefore maintained a kind of tripartite structure of loyalties: duty to the church (which was conceived as separate from, and transcending, temporal rulers), duty to the king, and loyalty and service to the lord of their locality. Often the sovereign and the lord had to resort to coercion when loyalty or service was withheld. The term 'nations' therefore had no political significance until the late 18th century. It simply meant, as Kedourie puts it, 'groups belonging together by similarity of birth, larger than a family but smaller than a clan or a people or places of provenance'.

The origins of modern political nationalism lie in the historical movements or trends in evidence in the Western European states of the 16th and 17th centuries, whereby the loyalty to the king and king's government became identified with, if not equated with, the overall interests of the ruler, his officials, and the entire population. Most important of all, when *raison d'état* and increasing cultural linguistic identification were reinforced by the economically maximizing potential of mercantilist, centralized, state government, the nation-state clearly emerged as the predominant and most viable European political unit.

The modern European political doctrines and movements of nationalism did not crystallize, however, until the French Revolution. It is primarily in the writings of Rousseau that we find the most powerful source of the recharging of the nation-state concept and the basis of nationalism as political doctrine. Rousseau and the Jacobins asserted the claims of the *whole population* to sovereignty over their state, for the first time proposing that the model state was synonymous with the nation.

Principles of national solidarity, universal citizenship, equal rights to civic participation and equal treatment under the law, all underpin the modern doctrine of nationalism. Once defined in terms of the entire population within a given territory, or a whole ethnic or linguistic group, nationalism asserts that the nation should become the fundamental and universal unit of political organization. Human society becomes a world of nation-states. The inevitable corollary (revolutionary, of course, in the context of 19th-century Europe) was that any nation that was oppressed by another had the right to be emancipated and made fully politically self-determining so that it could enjoy 'full nationhood'.

The nationalist doctrine has been attacked very effectively on three main fronts. The first practical point raised is that there

9. **The Paris Peace Conference redrew the map of Europe after the First World War. Critics argue that the Treaty of Versailles contained the seeds of the Second World War.**

is no clear agreement about how the nation should be defined. Linguistic, ethnic, and cultural-historical differences have an unfortunate habit of cross-cutting. The national determinationists in the Versailles settlement, for example, confronted ultimately insoluble difficulties in following this principle to its logical conclusions. Far from creating a new map of watertight 'pure' national units, the 1919 frontiers created fresh problems for the national minorities inconveniently trapped on the wrong sides of the new state boundaries.

Secondly, as Kedourie forcefully argues in *Nationalism*, the insistence of nationalists upon the right of national self-determination has often been mistaken by well-meaning Anglo-American liberals for a preference for constitutional democracy as a form of national self-government. Successive newly independent nation-states of the Middle East, Africa, and Asia have shown that independence in no way guarantees the adoption and maintenance of democratic free elections, parliamentary government, and independent judiciary or the protection of basic civil liberties in the state concerned.

The third point, which is the burden of E. H. Carr's brilliant short essay *Nationalism and After* (1945), is that the spread of nationalist doctrines and movements has, far from creating a happy family of nations, exacerbated international conflict. Indeed, nationalist doctrines have provided additional justification for revolution and war, have formed the basis for a popular commitment to, and involvement in, national struggles, and have provided a powerful political rationalization and propaganda instrument for indoctrinating mass armies and waging 'total war'.

On the other hand, nationalist doctrines are clearly not wholly responsible for the parlous state of international relations. Whatever Johann Gottlieb Fichte (1762–1814, German philosopher), Ernest Renan (1823–92, French theorist), and the sillier romantic dreams of nationalist propagandists in the 19th century may have claimed, most nationalist political leaders have shown realism in appreciating that the achievement of national political self-determination can neither eradicate all external dependence and obligations nor provide a universal elixir for world peace. When critics castigate nationalist doctrines for their aggressiveness and propensity for inducing political violence, they are generally confusing nationalism in its *pure form* with doctrines of racial supremacy or ideologies of imperial aggrandizement. Given the conjunction of the rise of the nation-state with the collapse of the absolute monarchy and the rise of republican democracy, was it not inevitable that the people of Europe should look to national identity and solidarity to provide a legitimation for political autonomy? Were Gladstone, Asquith, and Lloyd George (and Woodrow Wilson for that matter) so wrong to concede to Irishmen or Czechs or Poles the right to self-determination, freedom from an alien rule which their people had never endorsed or accepted? Surely it is natural justice that people who feel themselves part of a homogeneous national community should enjoy the dignity and status of national political autonomy, so long as it is admitted that such autonomy does not in itself resolve the pressing problems of internal political and economic justice, or the problem of creating a stable international order?

Major forms of nationalist movements

Cultural-linguistic nationalism

Many of the pioneers of Slav, Western European, Middle Eastern, and African political nationalisms were *literati* who used their writings to project their consciousness of national distinctiveness and develop their initial claim for political independence. Nationalist leaders and intellectuals, once independence is achieved, may be displaced by other revolutionary political forces. Nevertheless, the newly independent nations, like their long-established ex-imperial rulers, rapidly appreciate the importance of cultural nationalism ('the battle of the books') for the intensification of their own people's national commitments.

In cases of long-standing imperial control or attempted elimination of political nationalism, cultural nationalism stubbornly survives. As the former Soviet Union found, it is almost impossible, in practice, to eliminate the linguistic identity and solidarity of an ethnic group. Indeed there is strong evidence, in Ireland and Wales in the 19th century for example, that the more the native language of an ethnic group is despised and deliberately discouraged by a government, the more it gains in mystique and significance as a street language for the expression of communal sufferings and hopes. Where the tradition of culture and language is still widely disseminated among an entire ethnic community, it is entirely unrealistic, as was proved in the case of the Austro-Hungarian Empire in the 19th century, to hope to prevent a political phoenix arising from the embers of cultural nationalism simply by granting a limited imperial recognition of national cultural identity. Only when the larger proportion of an ethnic group has been assimilated in the politically dominant culture, as in modern Brittany, does cultural nationalism survive as a doomed minority movement tragically unable to extend its cultural-linguistic base sufficiently to capture power by democratic means.

Anti-colonial nationalism in the 'Third World'

Nationalism was originally a European political doctrine, and it developed in the Third World as a by-product of colonial experience, accompanying or following the impact of colonial rule rather than preceding it. Herculean efforts at nation-building therefore proceed simultaneously with the construction of the political and administrative apparatus of a modern state. In most cases, however, it is by the accidents of colonial inheritance that the territorial configuration and the designated population, as well as the official language, educational system, and the major economic and administrative institutions have been determined. In such a setting, the appeals of doctrines of national self-determination to a European-educated but partially alienated and subordinated intelligentsia were absolutely overwhelming. Here, couched in terms that Europeans found immediately comprehensible, was the very rationalization they needed for their claims to run their own affairs, liberated from imperialist rule. To carry through their objectives, however, they had to create a national identity, consciousness, and solidarity among their own people, a deep popular movement fired with a commitment to national independence. Not surprisingly, colonial governments at first attempted to crush such movements, though precise treatment varied according to the imperial power concerned and its political and military circumstances. A pragmatic colonialist tradition, such as the British, was able to engender policies of actually encouraging or conniving with the new nationalist movement in the belief that the colonial power could thus more effectively weld the often disparate and warring tribes and religious communities into a stable and orderly polity.

The early colonial nationalists, however, very soon found themselves threatened by the outflanking economic revolutionism of socialist and Marxist movements. Those leaders who clung to a vague populist appeal, to an abstract millennialism, or to dependence on their charismatic predominance, have frequently paid the price for failing to deliver the material goods, a greater social and economic equality, and improved living standards.

In many cases, especially in the British colonies, the colonial power's permissive rule encouraged the formation of nationalist parliamentary parties as a form of 'democratic tutelage', and where this happened the mass violence of a revolutionary overthrow of colonial rule was often avoided. In other circumstances, as in Cyprus, Algeria, and Aden, nationalist movements found themselves suppressed or outlawed by the colonial government, and resorted to extra-legal, underground, guerrilla, and resistance tactics in order to wrest control from their colonial rulers. Both revolutionary 'movements of national liberation' and essentially non-violent emergent nationalist parties require, above all, powerful bases of mass support and active participation if they are to wrest and hold power. The former type has to prove its popular legitimacy in the crucible of revolutionary war, and the latter has to prove its nationalist credentials to the departing power and to its own people. It should be stressed, however, that such movements may be far more ephemeral and unstable coalitions than has been assumed hitherto. Where such movements divide and collapse, the very possibility of a popularly legitimate regime, even the nascent sense of national identity and solidarity, may be lost. In such a vacuum the way is open to determined minority groups, particularly the military officers with a monopoly of control over the coercive forces of the state to snatch a *coup d'état*, rationalized as 'the maintenance of national unity' or 'preserving law and order'.

Multinational Corporations (MNCs)

The new Secretary of State will certainly need to be briefed about MNCs. They are among the most influential and powerful non-state actors in the international system. The largest MNCs are likely to possess assets and deploy annual budgets which dwarf those of the many poor states where their operations may be located. MNCs have grown rapidly since the economic recovery following the Second World War and have undoubtedly made a major contribution to the growth of the world economy. Because, by definition, MNCs operate simultaneously in several countries or in some cases numerous countries, they can choose to locate their operations in those parts of the world where it is most profitable. They also have access to considerable funds for investment and can command the best available business and technical expertise.

However, although many countries, especially developing countries, are generally eager to attract MNCs they often hopelessly overestimate the benefits to be gained. MNCs tend to use capital-intensive methods of production, in which case they will not need to employ large numbers of workers from the host country. Often the skilled and managerial employees will be brought in from overseas. They may manage to avoid the host country's taxation by the simple device of shifting the profits out of the host country. Often the MNCs exploit the offers of incentives by the host countries quite cynically, by taking the 'carrots' offered and then reconfiguring their operations in ways that deprive the host countries of benefit.

It is a common error, however, to assume that the MNC is 'sovereign' and that 'globalization' has destroyed the capacity of the state to strike back at MNCs when they wish to do so. States have ultimate control over their territories and borders. They can and do seize MNC assets, expel MNC personnel, nationalize MNCs, impose draconian fines and punishments for alleged violations of laws, and so on. Ultimately the state is still sovereign, though it may be reluctant to take extreme steps against an MNC for fear of causing a flight of overseas investment and the withdrawal of other MNCs from the country.

It will also be very hard for the new Secretary of State to resist MNC pressures on the US government to intervene on their behalf in the event of a major clash with the host state government. However, if the new Secretary of State is able to push through quietly policies that substantially assist the MNC she might hope to be offered an attractive non-executive directorship when she eventually retires from politics!

Guerrillas and insurgents

Guerrilla warfare is the natural weapon of the strategically weaker side in a conflict. Rather than risking the annihilation of their own forces in a full-scale battle with better armed and more numerous opponents, the guerrilla wages what Taber has called 'the war of the flea', using methods, times, and places of the guerrilla's choice and constantly striving to benefit from the guerrilla's major tactical advantage – the element of surprise. It is a classic method of warfare, almost as old as the history of human society.

A key lesson from the recent history of guerrilla warfare, as shown in a masterly survey by Walter Laqueur, *Guerrilla*, is that it is hardly ever a self-sufficient means of achieving victory. Only when the anti-guerrilla side underestimates the guerrilla threat, or simply fails to commit adequate resources to the conflict, does a guerrilla have a change of achieving, unaided, long-term political aims. In most 20th-century cases, guerrilla warfare on a major scale has been linked to revolutionary warfare, a struggle between a non-state movement (in some cases assisted or sponsored by a state) and a government for political and social control of a people in a given nation-state's territory. Most revolutionary wars (for example, in China, Vietnam, and Cambodia) have moved through a guerrilla phase and have finally developed into a decisive struggle between conventional armed forces. But the evidence from guerrilla struggles and revolutionary warfare in Latin America, where a number of attempts were made to emulate the success of Fidel Castro's guerrilla revolution in Cuba, shows that where there are determined and ruthless efforts to suppress them and the revolutionaries fail to gain substantial and lasting mass support, guerrilla campaigns will end in failure.

However, it would be a serious mistake to conclude that guerrilla warfare has become obsolete as a result of developments in military technology and counter-insurgency. Guerrilla warfare continues to prove effective in tying down large numbers of security forces, disrupting government and the economy: it poses a particularly serious threat to weak and unstable governments in divided societies. The protracted insurgency in Iraq, where rural

10. Vladimir Ilyich Lenin (1870–1924) founded the Bolshevik Party and the Marxist-Leninist ideology of the Soviet Union, which aimed at world revolution against 'capitalist imperialism' – a project which failed completely with the collapse of the Soviet Union.

and urban guerrilla attacks on the Coalition armed forces have been combined with major terrorist attacks against the civilian population, has killed hundreds of Coalition troops and members of the new Iraqi army and police, and thousands of civilians.

The newly appointed UK Foreign Secretary will need to convey these lessons to his Cabinet colleagues and to his opposite numbers in the US and the other NATO member states in the hope that they will not again be tempted into underestimating the challenges of major insurgencies and terrorism in future conflicts, and the implications for international relations. The consequences of all-out civil war in Iraq and the possible acquisition of a new base area by Al Qaeda in the midst of the Middle East would indeed have dire effects on international security and stability.

Terrorist groups and networks

Terrorism is the systematic use of coercive intimidation, usually to service political ends. It is used to create and exploit a climate of fear among a wider target group than the immediate victims of the violence and to publicize a cause, as well as to coerce a target into assenting to the terrorist aims. Terrorism may be used on its own or as part of a wider unconventional war. It can be employed by desperate and weak minorities, by states as a tool of domestic and foreign policy, or by belligerents as an accompaniment in all types and stages of warfare. A common feature is that innocent civilians, sometimes foreigners who know nothing of the terrorists' political quarrel, are killed or injured. Typical methods of modern terrorism are explosive and incendiary bombings, shooting attacks and assassinations, hostage-taking and kidnapping, and hijacking. The possibility of terrorists using nuclear, chemical, or bacteriological weapons cannot be discounted.

One basic distinction is between state and factional terror. The former has been vastly more lethal and has often been an antecedent to and a contributory cause of factional terrorism. Once regimes and factions decide that their ends justify any means or their opponents' actions justify them in unrestrained retaliation, they tend to become locked in a spiral of terror and counter-terror. Internal terrorism is confined within a single state or region while international terrorism, in its most obvious manifestation, is an attack carried out across international frontiers or against a foreign target in the terrorists' state of origin. But, in reality, most terrorism has international dimensions, as groups look abroad for support, weapons, and safe haven.

Terrorism is not a philosophy or a movement: it is a method. But even though we may be able to identify cases where terrorism has been used for causes most liberals would regard as just, this does not mean that even in such cases the use of terrorism, which by definition threatens the most fundamental rights of innocent civilians, is morally justified. Paradoxically, despite the rapid growth in the incidence of modern terrorism, this method has been remarkably unsuccessful in gaining strategic objectives. The only clear cases are the expulsion of British and French colonial rule from Palestine, Cyprus, Aden, and Algeria. The continuing popularity of terrorism among nationalists and ideological and religious extremists must be explained by other factors: the craving for physical expression of hatred and revenge; terrorism's record of success in yielding tactical gains (e.g. massive publicity, release of prisoners, and large ransom payments); and the fact that the method is relatively cheap, easy to organize, and carries minimal risk. Regimes of totalitarianism, such as Nazism and Stalinism, routinely used mass terror to control and persecute whole populations, and the historical evidence shows that this is a tragically effective way of suppressing opposition and resistance. But when states use international terrorism they invariably seek to disguise their role, possibly denying responsibility for specific crimes. Another major conducive factor in the growth of modern terrorism has been repeated weakness and appeasement in national and international reaction to terrorism, despite numerous anti-terrorist laws and conventions and much governmental rhetoric. Early writings on terrorism tended to treat it as a relatively minor threat to law and order and individual human rights. In a series of studies, for example, *Terrorism and the Liberal State*, I concluded that major outbreaks of terrorism, because of their capacity to affect public opinion and foreign policy and to trigger civil and international wars, ought to be recognized as a potential danger to the security and well-being of afflicted states and a possible threat to international peace.

There are of course many other threats and challenges which are potentially far more serious than terrorism. Global climate change, the existence of which has been scientifically proven to the satisfaction of all but a curious group of flat-earthers, could bring catastrophic changes. Scientists are also concerned about the dangers of a global pandemic which could kill hundreds of thousands of people. Despite the efforts to maintain a global nuclear non-proliferation regime, proliferation continues and the IAEA (International Atomic Energy Agency) estimates that there are over 40 states capable of using their civil nuclear technology and resources to pursue nuclear weapons programmes. I will consider some of these global problems in Chapter 4.

In view of these potential dangers it would be wrong to exaggerate the danger from international terrorism, but what any Foreign Minister will need to understand is that the so-called New Terrorism of the Al Qaeda network of networks is the most dangerous type of international terrorism ever experienced from a non-state entity in the international system. Why is this?

First, Al Qaeda is explicitly aiming at the mass killing of civilians. Al Qaeda declared a jihad or holy war against the US and its allies. In bin Laden's so-called 'fatwa' of 23 February 1998, he announced the setting up of a World Islamic Front for Jihad and declared that it is 'the duty of all Muslims to kill US citizens – civilian or military and their allies everywhere'. The readiness to kill civilians on a massive scale was demonstrated in the attacks of 11 September 2001 which caused the deaths of nearly 3,000 people.

Second, the Al Qaeda network has a presence in over 60 countries and this makes it the most widely dispersed international terrorist network ever experienced in the history of terrorism. Al Qaeda's large number of affiliates and operational and support network not only gives a genuine global reach to their terrorist activities, it also enables them to claim with some truth that they are continuing to wage a 'global jihad'. Indeed, Al Qaeda is more of a global transnational movement bound together mainly by a shared ideology than a traditional highly centralized organization.

Typical current Al Qaeda methods are no-warning coordinated suicide attacks hitting several targets simultaneously. Al Qaeda's

11. **The twin towers of New York's World Trade Center on fire after being struck by airliners seized by Al Qaeda suicide hijackers on 11 September 2001.**

most commonly used weapon has been the large suicide vehicle bomb. However, the Al Qaeda network has shown a keen interest in obtaining weapons of mass destruction (WMD). Its track record shows that it would have no compunction about using them to cause large numbers of civilian deaths.

Now let us turn from one of the most malevolent non-states to the most benevolent.

Humanitarian and human rights organizations

There is an impressive array of humanitarian organizations and charities which operate internationally and which bring great dedication, skill, and experience to bear in order to save lives, alleviate suffering, and assist in post-disaster relief and reconstruction. Among the best known of these organizations are the International Red Cross, Médecins Sans Frontières, Oxfam, Save the Children Fund, and Christian Aid, but there are many others.

Most of the international relief work done by these organizations is delivered in the form of humanitarian assistance, with the full consent of the authorities in the country in need. They have made a huge contribution to provision of relief even in the most daunting of humanitarian crisis situations, such as the Indian Ocean Tsunami (2004) and the Pakistan Earthquake disaster (2005). Governments in stricken countries simply cannot cope in the face of large-scale disasters. Assistance rendered by other governments is very important but it could never be enough. What the non-state humanitarian organizations can bring to bear very rapidly in such situations is local knowledge and contacts with the affected communities, great experience of delivering humanitarian

12. Relief workers delivering humanitarian aid to an area devastated by the huge tsunami caused by a submarine earthquake on 26 December 2004 – it struck coasts as far away as Sri Lanka and Thailand, killing an estimated 150,000 people.

aid, and the help of professional experts such as doctors, nurses and so on, and (usually) wide experience of working with host governments and intergovernmental organizations such as the UN agencies.

Far more controversial is the growing trend towards coercive intervention, that is intervention without the consent of the target country's government. Examples are the establishing of Kurdish 'safe havens' in northern Iraq (1991), plus interventions in Somalia, Haiti, Liberia, Rwanda, and Bosnia. This trend has been facilitated by the gradual weakening of the principle of state sovereignty; the growth of human rights awareness; the propensity of the UN Security Council to widen the concept of 'threat to the peace'; and the globalization of information.

Yet despite the gradual undermining of the principle of absolute state sovereignty, there are considerable countervailing pressures in the international system which still constitute major obstacles to coercive humanitarian intervention: there is the fear that such intervention might provoke a breakdown of international order; states may also be reluctant to commit themselves to intervention because they fear that it may turn into a very costly long-term responsibility with no prospect of an easy exit; there is the worry of regimes, particularly in the developing countries, that intervention might become a cover for the major powers to interfere in their affairs.

Non-state organizations have the huge advantage that they do not engender the sort of mistrust and concern caused by the intervention of foreign states. Non-state humanitarian organizations seem likely to continue to play a vital part in delivering relief to countries with humanitarian crises. Enlightened governments should welcome the NGOs' contribution and be ready to develop fuller dialogue and cooperation with them in order to help them to optimize their capacity to deliver their knowledge, resources, and specialized skills directly to the populations that are in greatest need.

Human rights organizations such as Human Rights Watch and Amnesty International have a similarly vital role. Few governments would be prepared to speak so openly to condemn human rights violations. Governments tend to be worried about losing lucrative trade or investment opportunities or access to key commodities such as oil or natural gas. Non-state human rights organizations can perform an invaluable role by educating and mobilizing international opinion and shaming governments that abuse human rights by spreading accurate information about their misdeeds.

How would a senior adviser sum up his briefing to a new Secretary of State or a new Foreign Secretary on non-states? If he is doing his job properly he will avoid the old canard of state-centrism. He will not try to suggest that non-states can be safely ignored. States are extremely important, but so also are many non-state phenomena.

The new Secretary of State will ignore them at her peril. Let us bear in mind that non-state organizations succeed in seizing power in Russia in 1917, in China in 1949, in India in 1948, and in Iran in 1979, and it was a non-state organization/network that carried out the devastating attacks on 11 September 2001. As a result of the actions of Al Qaeda on 9/11 we have a 'War on Terror', the war in Iraq, and a war in Afghanistan. It would be absurd to claim that non-state organizations are of only peripheral importance and have had no significant impact on international relations.

Chapter 3

Intergovernmental organizations (IGOs)

Varieties of IGOs

IGOs are a special category of international organizations.
In the previous chapter we considered a number of
non-governmental international organizations (NGOs), some of
which have had a major impact on international relations. IGOs
are always founded by governments which recognize that it is in
their national interests to obtain multilateral agreements and
pursue actions to deal with threats, challenges, or problems that
cannot be dealt with effectively at the unilateral level. This kind
of international cooperation between states is not a new idea.
The Concert of Powers established in Europe in the aftermath
of the Napoleonic Wars was a striking illustration of the major
European powers collaborating on a long-term basis in order to
try to preserve international order and the security interests of
the states that belonged to the system. It may have lacked the
grandiose constitutional frameworks of the League of Nations and
the United Nations but it did help the major powers to sustain
a relatively stable balance of power in Europe and to prevent
a major European war for over half a century. The key to this
success was that it reflected rather than defied the reality of the
balance of power in Europe at that time. As we will observe later,
this was in contrast with the League of Nations, which failed to
reflect the balance of power from its inception to its early demise.

There are two key dimensions which are valuable in any comparative analysis of IGOs. The first is the *scope* of the IGO, by which I mean the number of issue areas it can influence in international relations. The second is the *domain* of the IGO, meaning the number of states and significant non-state organizations over which it is able to exert influence. The United Nations is the extreme example: it has scope over an almost limitless range of issue areas and potential issue areas, and its domain includes almost every state in the world today. However, the sheer range of the scope and its near comprehensive domain have meant that it has always been seriously constrained in what it can actually achieve, not least because it is composed of independent sovereign states, including the most powerful states in the world, far beyond the capacity of the UN to dominate or control, and because it is dependent on the concerted support and the economic and military resources of its key member states (the US and the other four permanent members of the UN Security Council – Russia, China, the UK, and France) in order to implement its policies.

In complete contrast there are numerous functional IGOs established to deal with narrowly defined special functions. This type of IGO is sometimes assumed to be an ultra-modern development, but in fact some were established in the 19th century. Probably the first of these specialized functional IGOs was the Central Commission for the Navigation of the Rhine set up in 1815. A more recent (20th-century) example is the International Police Organization, better known by its acronym, INTERPOL, an association of over 100 national police forces devoted to fighting international crime.

One category of IGO which expanded very rapidly in the 20th century is the regional IGO, including the European Union (EU), the Organization of American States (OAS), and the Association of South East Asian Nations (ASEAN). These IGOs were formed to strengthen cooperation by states at regional level. Not all these regional organizations are committed to developing full-scale regional integration or even partial integration. The European Union is the only IGO which has managed to achieve a relatively high level of economic integration. Most of its member states are now committed to using the euro, a common currency designed for all EU states. By contrast the OAS and ASEAN have not advanced very far beyond improved intergovernmental economic discussions and cooperation on issues on which they agree. An important variety of IGO is the special interest organization which has a very specific issue area and a domain which crosses all regional boundaries. A good example is the Organization of Petroleum Exporting Countries (OPEC).

Last but not least there are IGOs which have been established with the objective of promoting regional security. The North Atlantic Treaty Organization (NATO) is the best known of these but there are also the Organization for Security and Cooperation in Europe (OSCE) and the Australia, New Zealand and US Security Treaty group (ANZUS), and other security groupings elsewhere in the world. NATO is far and away the most powerful and integrated of these regional military security organizations. The fact that its leading member state is the sole remaining superpower is the reason why it is so militarily powerful. NATO's *raison d'être* when it was founded in 1949 was to provide a strong defensive alliance to protect the whole North Atlantic area, including all Western Europe, against possible military expansion by the Soviet Union. One might have thought that NATO would disappear with the ending of the cold war, but far from fading away, the Alliance has actually increased its membership by admitting East European countries such as Poland, Hungary, and the Czech Republic which were able to liberate themselves from communist rule at the end of the cold war. NATO, OSCE, and the other regional defence organizations are legitimate IGOs under the UN Charter. However, many critics of the recent expansion of NATO argue NATO's move into Eastern Europe, formerly part of the Soviet sphere of influence, has been a key factor in motivating President Putin to pursue a major rearmament programme and to deploy anti-ballistic missiles. This is once again an illustration of the 'security dilemma' at work, slowing down or halting major disarmament efforts and refuelling arms races. Whatever the rights and wrongs of this controversy, it is abundantly clear that, as a result of the US role as the dominant power in the Alliance and the organization's long experience of operating a properly integrated command structure, it is by far the most powerful alliance in the world today. The differences between the US and key NATO European allies, France and Germany, over the invasion of Iraq undoubtedly created tensions within the Alliance but did not undermine its effectiveness. NATO is now providing a valuable contribution in Afghanistan where President Karzai and his democratic government confront a difficult security situation with the Taliban in collaboration with some local warlords attempting to regain control in parts of the east and south-east of the country. European members of the Alliance undoubtedly recognize the organisation's great value as a guarantor of their future security, but some politicians and senior military figures do express concern that the US may at some stage grow weary of its NATO commitments and withdraw into a 'fortress America' posture. There has been a current of US neo-isolationism in the not so distant past, for example, in the 1930s, and any repetition of this withdrawal from the task of preserving international security would certainly have serious consequences. Most NATO European allies are entirely dependent on the Alliance for their nuclear deterrent shield. *All* European NATO allies are dependent on the US for the airlift and sealift capabilities essential for any significant overseas operations. It should be recalled that NATO would have been severely limited in its capacity to act in the Balkans crisis concerning Bosnia and Kosovo in the 1990s had it not been for the Clinton administration's belated but crucial decision to help to find a lasting solution to the ethnic cleansing and other brutal violations of human rights in the former Yugoslavia. 'Why couldn't the European Union have acted?' asked the newly appointed Foreign

Secretary. The Permanent Under-Secretary smiles indulgently at his new boss before replying, like a schoolmaster trying to deal with a pupil who is well intentioned but rather slow on the uptake.

> The EU is not what one might describe as a security organization. The only kind of security the EU parliamentarians and European Commission civil servants are really interested in is social security. They keep on talking about a European Army, and a common Europe and Security Policy, but the EU has no special knowledge in the defence field. It has no experience of deploying forces effectively as a regional IGO. It is a quintessentially *civilian* organization and its member states have always been able to sit back and allow NATO and the US ally to take care of any military security issues. I would respectfully suggest, Foreign Secretary, that you maintain closest possible links with NATO and, above all, keep the US government fully committed to its leadership role in the Alliance. Not that I mean we should downgrade our attention to EU matters – it is just a question of horses for courses. NATO for our long-term security, the EU for a remarkably attractive market for goods and services even if one has to admit that since the latest EU enlargement it is too cumbersome to make sensible decisions at a sensible speed.

At this point in the briefing the Permanent Under-Secretary might think it better not to launch into a detailed account of the byzantine complexities of the EU's institutions and processes and how some of its member states were seriously convinced that they could resurrect the European Constitution that had already been decisively rejected by French and Dutch voters in summer 2005. He could see the new Foreign Secretary's eyes glazing over. There would be another time to reveal the mysteries of the EU to his new boss.

In the mean time the more urgent task was to brief him about the only world IGO we have got, the United Nations, its weaknesses and its hidden strengths – so well hidden in fact that many of the new Foreign Secretary's opposite numbers were going to send deputies to represent them at the next UN conference in New York. However, before tackling the UN aspect of the Foreign Secretary's job it might be helpful to review the brief, brave but (as the Permanent Under-Secretary might see it) naïve and totally misguided experiment of the League of Nations, the precursor of the UN and putative world institution for preventing any repetition of the horrific tragedy of the First World War. The story of the League is an essential lesson in the dangers of misguided idealism in international relations to which all foreign ministers and heads of government should be exposed.

The League of Nations

The First World War (1914–18) was a colossal tragedy for humanity. Not only did it cause millions of deaths and terrible injuries among participants on all sides: it also set in train the events which appeared ineluctably to lead to the even greater tragedy of the rise of Nazism and the Second World War.

The First World War was a tragedy in the true sense: it could have been avoided if the quality of leadership of the major powers had been adequate to the task of proper diplomatic communication and negotiation. It was like a gigantic railway accident in which the drivers were blindly rushing ahead without thought for the possible consequences of the collision. This metaphor is not inappropriate because the means by which Germany and the other major belligerents set in motion their mobilization of troops for war was the railways. The historian, A. J. P. Taylor made an important point in his book *The First World War* when he wrote: 'The First World War had begun – imposed on the statesmen of Europe by railway timetables. It was an unexpected climax to the railway age.'

It is literally true that by the time the wiser heads tried to intervene to warn of the dangers of war and to stop the mobilizations it was too late: the trains were moving out of the stations across Europe. There was so little understanding of the likely consequences of a full-scale European war that flag-waving crowds went to cheer the troops as they departed, and the public believed the war would be over by Christmas. They did not foresee the nightmarish horrors of trench warfare and mass bombardments that wiped out millions of young lives. One only has to visit the war memorials in the villages, towns, and churches of the United Kingdom, France, and other belligerents to realize that a whole generation was decimated by the war. Small wonder that the popular slogans at the end of the conflict were that it was 'the War to end Wars' and it was 'making the world safe for democracy'.

President Woodrow Wilson, the US leader who had reluctantly taken America into the war, was desperately keen to ensure that in the post-war peace settlement a new world organization would be established which would be able to ensure perpetual peace. He was the statesman most committed to the idea of a League of Nations when the victorious powers met at Versailles to decide the terms of peace. It was Wilson's energy and commitment to the idea of a League, an idea which had been discussed and proposed by many idealistic people, including Jan Smuts of South Africa, Leonard Woolf, and many liberal intellectuals, which forced it onto the Versailles agenda, despite the fact that Clemenceau was deeply sceptical and Lloyd George was only lukewarm about the idea.

The League was undoubtedly the most daring and innovative proposal to reshape international relations to have been put forward in the early 20th century. The League Covenant and the major organs of the new organization were aimed at establishing procedures for the peaceful resolution of international conflicts and disputes. The League was to have three main organs:

a Council of 15 member states, including the United Kingdom, France, and the Soviet Union as permanent members, which would meet three times a year; an Assembly in which all member states would be represented and which would meet annually; and a permanent Secretariat. A key principle of the League was that all decisions had to be by unanimous vote. Needless to say this made it very difficult, indeed well nigh impossible, for the League to act swiftly and effectively in times of international crisis. It was an underlying assumption that the League would intervene in international conflicts. Parties to disputes were supposed to put their complaints before the League or to international arbitrators, but if the League or arbitration could not reach a decision the parties to the dispute could go to war after a further pause of three months. The Permanent Court of International Justice could also become involved.

In theory the key article of the League Covenant was supposed to be No. 16 which enabled the League to invoke economic or military sanctions against a defiant state. In practice every member state could decide whether they wished to participate in economic or military sanctions.

This convoluted procedure and weak constitution partly explains why the League proved to be so useless in the face of Italian, German, and Japanese aggression in the 1930s. But the major reason for the abject failure of the League to uphold international peace and security was that it did not reflect the realities of the balance of power in the inter-war period.

Paradoxically the United States Congress refused to agree to America joining the League despite the fact that President Woodrow Wilson was the major champion of the idea at Versailles. The absence of the US was of huge significance because it deprived the League of America's military and economic power. Germany, Japan, and Italy, under their dictatorships, rejected the authority of the League. One of Hitler's most popular rallying cries during the Nazis' rise to power was his denunciation of the 'diktat' of the Versailles Treaty. When the League failed again to stop Italian aggression in Abyssinia, Japanese aggression in Manchuria, Hitler's seizure of the Ruhr, Hitler's Anschluss with Austria, and Hitler's invasion of Czechoslovakia, it was clear that it was a broken reed.

Despite its failure to maintain peace and security, however, the League did at least provide evidence of a desire to establish an international institution capable of maintaining peace. In this sense it paved the way for the UN, and readers will note in the next section that the framers of the UN Charter borrowed some elements of League structure in designing the new world IGO. Fortunately, as we shall see in the next section, the founders of the UN had much greater realism than the providers of the League. Hence, despite its obvious weaknesses, the UN has shown much greater durability than its predecessor and has always been able to exert more influence, not primarily in the peace and security task but in the whole range of specialist agencies which have done remarkable work in assisting in the economic development of less developed countries, promoting world health, providing emergency care for refugees, and so on. These achievements are not minor: they constitute a major contribution to international relations. Nevertheless, on peace and security issues the UN stands to be judged almost as harshly as the League. Let us consider why this should be so. Did we not learn lessons from the League?

The United Nations

Although the political leaders of the Allies in the Second World War recognized the need for a new world organization to replace the failed League of Nations and the UN Charter does constitute a considerable advance on the League Covenant in many respects, the UN labours under similar grave disadvantages when it attempts to carry out its major task of ensuring world peace

and security. As was the League, the UN is founded on the twin
principles of the sovereignty of states and an essentially voluntary
system of collective security, meaning that the organization has no
means of enforcing its decisions and it is up to the member states
themselves to decide what their obligations to the UN should
be and whether they should honour them. These fundamental
weaknesses are simply an inescapable consequence of the
quasi-anarchic nature of international relations. There is no world
sovereign body because states believe that the creation of a world
government with the power and the authority to make and enforce
world laws would sometimes work against their national interests.

Thus, while it is true that the UN Charter gives the world
organization stronger powers than the League had under the
Covenant, it has failed time and again when confronting major
threats to peace and security. However, when I say the UN has
failed I am really criticizing the member states, for it is *they* who
decide (or fail to decide) what, if anything, the UN should do.

It is therefore a mistake to judge the UN as an autonomous actor
in the international system: it is in essence an intergovernmental
forum constantly constrained by basic inter-state disagreements
and disputes both in the Security Council and the General
Assembly.

The UN Charter is the world organization's basic constitution
and a major source of international law. It defines the aims of
the UN very broadly indeed: maintaining international peace
and security by means of peaceful settlement of disputes and
collective security; the promotion of international cooperation in
the economic and social fields; and the promotion of respect for
universal human rights. It is important to bear in mind that the
Charter confers duties as well as rights on member states.

The vagueness of the Charter's language and underlying principles
has turned out to be one of the UN's hidden strengths, providing

it with far more flexibility and potential durability than the Covenant could ever provide for the League. For example, as F. H. Hinsley (1963), E. Luard (1979), and others, have pointed out, the decision to give each permanent member of the Security Council the power of veto gravely restricted its scope to influence events during the cold war. On the other hand, this provision in the UN Charter made it less likely that the major powers would withdraw from the organization, possibly leading to its ultimate fragmentation and demise.

The multilateral treaty that we know as the UN Charter emerged from the discussions at the Dumbarton Oaks and San Francisco Conferences at the end of the Second World War. It created six major UN institutions: the Security Council, containing major powers as permanent members and key executive decision-making powers to deal with crises such as threats to international and security; the General Assembly, an annual forum of all the member states' representatives which has responsibility for supervising all the other agencies which are part of the UN family (e.g. the World Health Organization (WHO), the Food and Agricultural Organization (FAO), and the UN Educational, Scientific and Cultural Organization (UNESCO); the UN Secretariat, headed by the Secretary-General; the Economic and Social Council, the forum for all the specialized functional agencies dealing with welfare and economic and social development issues; the International Court of Justice; and the Trusteeship Council which was set up to supervise non-self-governing territories designated by the UN as Trust Territories).

It is widely agreed among academic students of international relations and practitioners such as diplomats and legislators that the UN, due to factors beyond its control, has a very poor record in its attempts to maintain peace and security, and this situation has continued, despite the ending of the cold war. It has made a modest but useful contribution by deploying UN peace-keeping forces under the UN Security Council's mandate to help establish and maintain ceasefire and truce agreements and to help back up the diplomacy of conflict resolution. Peace-keeping is not mentioned in the UN Charter, but it has been a useful form of improvisation by the UN and, in a number of cases, it has helped to terminate conflicts (in Cyprus, the former Yugoslavia, Congo, for example). For the first 45 years of the UN's existence the UN Security Council (UNSC), consisting of 15 members (including the five permanent members), was virtually paralysed by the cold war ideological divisions between the US, UK, and France, on the one hand, and the former Soviet Union, on the other. All permanent members have the power of veto, and this made it all too easy for the former Soviet Union to block any Security Council resolution to which they were opposed. Therefore, although in theory the Security Council was given far stronger executive powers than the old League Council, they were practically useless during the cold war period. The only time the UNSC was able to authorize military action under Chapter VII of the UN Charter was to dispatch troops to South Korea to resist the North Korean invasion, but this was due simply to the absence of the Soviet delegate, and was of doubtful legality.

Despite the many severe setbacks the UN has suffered in its attempts to carry out its tasks of maintaining peace and security, many observers would give the UN system very high marks for the work of its specialized agencies. Indeed those who favour a 'functionalist' approach to international relations would argue that it is precisely through this cooperation on non-political matters, such as economic development and capacity-building in less developed countries, that states begin to act and develop a genuinely international society capable of pursuing the common interests of humankind.

The Permanent Under-Secretary in his briefings to the new UK Foreign Secretary would be unlikely to subscribe to this idealistic functionalist view. He would be in favour of the UK encouraging

13. The UN Security Council in session: it was established under the UN Charter as the permanent body to maintain peace and security and consists of five permanent members (US, Russia, China, UK, and France) and ten non-permanent members.

and assisting in the excellent work of the specialized agencies, but he would point out that there is no evidence to date that cooperation of this kind makes cooperation on peace and security issues any easier.

UN reform?

As has just been observed, the effect of cold war hostility and suspicion on the work of the Security Council was crippling so far as its role in maintaining international peace and security was concerned. With the ending of the cold war a window of opportunity for UN reform appeared to have opened. The UN provided major support for the liberation of Kuwait from the Iraqi invaders, and many observers hoped that a New International Order was being established, in which the UN had a vital and much more powerful role.

Sadly this opportunity was lost, and in the 1990s the world organization found itself hopelessly overstretched as a result of increasing efforts at humanitarian and peace-keeping responsibilities in a growing number of internal rather than inter-state conflicts, for example, in El Salvador, Haiti, Rwanda, Burundi, Mozambique, Angola, Liberia, and strife in the republics of the former Soviet Union and the former Yugoslavia.

The UN suffered severe setbacks in these conflicts: UN troops were taken hostage in Bosnia; the UN was compelled to withdraw from Somalia where the US troops had suffered casualties. In Rwanda, Burundi and other places, such as Darfur, where severe inter-communal wars are going on, the UN has often been stymied by lack of troops, shortage of funds, and disagreements among the UN Security Council members which have severely limited the UN's capability to intervene effectively. The work of the specialized agencies has continued to have truly remarkable results, despite the inadequate funding they receive for their crucial tasks.

Prime Minister Tony Blair is one political leader who has recently expressed his strong commitment to UN reform. It is clear that he sees no contradictions between this view and his belief that it was right to join with the United States in an invasion and occupation of Iraq, despite the failure of the US and the UK to gain explicit UN support for their military venture, and his confidence that the war was entirely justified and that the only 'mistakes' he and President Bush need to apologize for were errors in implementing the policy on Iraq.

In a speech at Georgetown University in 2006, Tony Blair argued for an enlargement of the UN Security Council, and appeared to sympathize with the demands of countries such as India, Brazil, Japan, and Germany for seats on the Security Council. He is also in favour of abolishing the veto powers of the permanent members of the Security Council. Moreover, and somewhat surprisingly, he has implied that the only way to overcome the unwillingness of other permanent member states to give up their veto powers would be for Britain to make the first step and give up its veto power.

But when one considers the likelihood of other permanent members, especially the US, Russia, and China, giving up their veto powers it seems more likely that the UK would simply be throwing aside its veto power in an empty gesture. Giving up the UK's veto power might, in some circumstances, constitute a grossly irresponsible step towards weakening the country's capacity to influence.

Tony Blair also proposed in his speech in Washington (on 26 May 2006) a strengthening of the role of the UN Secretary-General and a major reform of the UN's bureaucracy. None of these proposals for structural change in the UN is new. What was new in Tony Blair's speech was his proposal for enhancing the UN's capacity to take 'pre-emptive' action which has a distinctly neo-conservative ring. He said that the crisis in Darfur proved that the UN should be 'an empowered international actor', with the capacity to intervene militarily in undemocratic countries to spread democratic values around the world. One only has to consider the number of states that would feel threatened by the UN 'reformed' to conform to the Blair model to see why a reform of the UN on these grandiose lines appears highly unlikely. It is not only small and medium-sized states that would feel threatened by such changes. Large and important countries such as China and Russia would also be deeply opposed. A clear illustration of their very different concepts of the national interest is their opposition to international sanctions, especially military sanctions being used to force Iran to abandon its uranium enrichment programme. Beijing and Moscow have very different visions of a reformed 'world order' from those of Messrs Bush and Blair. The UN system has been able to endure so long because it has learnt to *manage* these often fundamental differences and to act as a genuinely *neutral* world organization. A sure way of undermining the UN and ultimately killing it off would be to force a straitjacket of control by the sole global superpower and its close allies.

Efforts to impose a single set of values or a particular ideology, religion, or political system on the world have almost invariably had tragic consequences. Better to have a UN system which acts as an effective forum and as a system for global diplomatic communication than a more powerful UN obtained at the cost of turning the world organization into an authoritarian world government or quasi-imperial system. And in an age of weapons of mass destruction the UN should surely be devoted to the prevention of war not to its promotion.

European Union

'European Union' is in some ways a rather misleading label for the complex of institutions and processes which are all part of the efforts by some Europeans to achieve European and economic and political integration. The decisive rejection of the draft European Union constitution by the French on 29 May 2005, and by the Dutch on 1 June 2005, shocked the European politicians and officials who wanted to move towards ever closer integration. Any EU Treaty has to be ratified by all member states before it can be put into force. It is particularly worrying for supporters of closer European integration that the two countries where the public rejected the draft constitution were founding member states in the European Economic Community which was set up in 1957. Moreover, six other member states (Britain, Ireland, Denmark, Sweden, the Czech Republic, and Poland) announced that they had no intention of holding referenda on the draft.

In the light of the current profound crisis over the future of the European integration project it is important to remind ourselves of the very special circumstances which attracted many of

Europe's political elite and business and professional groups to support the idea from the outset. The European nation-states had been devastated and impoverished by two world wars in the space of 50 years. They feared that if they remained divided on national lines they would be weak and potentially vulnerable to Soviet communist expansion. They also believed that European recovery would be stronger and swifter if they could achieve progress towards greater European economic integration.

A second powerful political motivation for developing economic integration was the belief that if you could integrate certain key sectors of the economy across national borders you would be able to reduce the war potential of states. The creation of the European Coal and Steel Community (ECSC) in 1951 was a major catalyst in the integration process. (Europeans recalled Hitler's exploitation of the key coalmining and industrial region, the Ruhr, between the wars.)

The idea of a coal and steel community had been proposed by the Schuman Plan in 1950 and was formally established by the Treaty of Paris (1951). It was a huge success and convinced the founding members (France, the Federal Republic of Germany, Italy, Belgium, the Netherlands, and Luxembourg) that they should take further steps towards European integration. Functionalists saw the success of integration of specific industrial sectors as confirmation of their belief that integration of non-political activities would ultimately facilitate political integration.

The functionalists' project of sectoral integration was greatly assisted by the success of ECSC. Further progress in this direction was seen in the establishment of the European Economic Community (EEC) and the European Atomic Community (EURATOM) by the Treaty of Rome in 1957. Further support for the functionalist approach as the most effective route to wider integration seemed to be provided by the complete failure of schemes to establish a Political Community and a European

Defence Community. But the attainment of greater economic integration in a growing number of economic sectors has not inevitably led to political integration. It was the *economic* success of the European integration sectoral functionalist model which was confirmed by the European Coal and Steel Community. Economies of scale could be achieved and access to greater investment and enhanced competitiveness provided the real engine of both European economic growth and the integrationist efforts, with all the founder members prospering greatly from their access to a wider European market.

It was the attraction of gaining access to the European Community (EC) Market that eventually attracted the United Kingdom to join the EC along with Denmark and Ireland in 1973. Greece joined in 1981 and Spain and Portugal in 1986. When the cold war ended it became possible for the states that had pursued a policy of strict neutrality in the cold war (Austria, Sweden, and Finland) to join, which they did in 1995. Once again, the primary motive in the case of every applicant country was *economic*.

The collapse of the former Soviet Union and the end of the cold war meant that there were no perceived military security benefits to be gained from the European Union. In any case, the security of the European Union democracies during the cold war was guaranteed by the NATO shield, incorporating the huge military resources of the United States for the collective security of the entire North Atlantic Treaty area.

It is a strange irony that, although the East European states accepted into the EU in the latest enlargement have joined primarily to gain the economic benefits of members – such as access to the largest single market in the world, the free movement of people, goods, and services across European borders, access to regional development grants, and so on – some awkward facts appear to be undermining hopes of an imminent European economic recovery.

Economic growth has been disappointingly sluggish. Unemployment is high in the member states and it appears to be difficult to bring these levels down. This applies just as much to the founding members as it does to some of the new ones. In France, Italy, and Germany, annual growth between 2001 and 2005 was only 0.9 per cent, compared to 2.6 per cent in the same period in Spain and Britain. Economic experts point to the urgent need for the EU to deregulate its labour markets and services. Above all, if the EU is to recover the economic success of its early years, it must work hard to prevent member states from using economic nationalism as an excuse for protection and for circumventing the tight EU competition rules. Determination to uphold the single market and to boost the freedom of movement of labour, goods, services, and capital is vital to the long-term health of the EU. The single market should provide the necessary foundation for the kind of economic recovery which would help to restore the EU's popularity and its confidence and sense of purpose.

However, to repeat an important lesson drawn from my overview of the UN, we should beware of placing all the blame for the EU's current woes and apparent loss of a sense of direction on the EU institutions. The EU is after all an IGO, though admittedly an unusual IGO in that it has carried regional economic integration efforts much further than any other regional organisation in the world. As an IGO the EU depends on its member states' governments and political leadership to make the organization's key decisions and to shape and implement its policies. The parliamentary democracies of Italy and Germany have experienced considerable political difficulties in the aftermath of very tight general elections and this has undoubtedly affected the ability of the new governments to act decisively and swiftly. The 'no' votes in the French and Dutch referenda on the EU constitution were almost certainly based on growing criticisms of the EU and on frustration and disillusion with their own governments in Paris and The Hague for their widely perceived failures to tackle the problems of lack of growth and lack of jobs in their own countries.

Yet, although it is stretching it too far to describe the EU as a fully autonomous actor in international relations, its achievements as an IGO working for the benefit of Europe are frequently underestimated. One major benefit the EU has brought to Europe is the consolidation of stability and democracy within applicant countries. By insisting that all applicant member states must have fully operative democratic political systems upholding the rule of law, respect for human rights, a functioning market economy, and adherence to EU rules, before they can be admitted, the EU has been an enormous influence for good. The largely unforeseen consequence of the massive enlargement of the EU is probably the most important effect that this ambitious IGO has had on international relations – it has made Europe more democratic.

Talk of rejecting applicant countries even after they have met the conditions required by the EU seems highly irresponsible. The fears of some member states that the economic consequences of enlargement will do serious harm to the EU have turned out to be groundless. The European Commission investigated this issue recently and found that the admission of new member states from Central Europe in 2004 had increased economic growth and created employment not only in the new member countries but also for existing members. We also need to bear in mind the likely consequences of refusing to admit new member states which have satisfied all the admission criteria. A recent special report by *The Economist* warned:

> Analysts of the western Balkans agree that if Brussels were to slam the door, these countries could easily slip back into nationalism, drug and people-smuggling, organised crime and even war – with lots of undesirable consequences for Western Europe. Similarly, a Turkey spurned by Europe could soon regress into a sour and militant Islamist mood, right on Europe's front line.

To conclude this brief discussion of the role of the EU, I will focus on two key trends which, whether the founder member states like it or not, are likely to determine the future shape of the European integration project. First, there is the far-reaching effect of enlargement. The current EU has four times the membership of the original European Economic Community. There is no sign that the new East European members are committed to supranationalism, on the contrary, having suffered decades of suffocating oppression under Soviet satellite communist regimes, they have a strong determination to enjoy having their own independent national governments.

The supranationalist politicians in the European Parliament, the European Commission, and some of the EU government are likely to discover that a 25-member-strong EU cannot be forced into a supranational structure. The EU will remain a crucially important forum and structure for closer European regional cooperation, but it is unlikely to become the equivalent of a United States of Europe. If the EU attempts to try to resurrect the draft European constitution and make the French and the Dutch vote on it again it is likely that it will only intensify the public opposition to the integration project. Europeans still identify their nation-state as the primary focus of their loyalty. National governments and parliaments are the institutions that Europeans still regard as the centres of power which they need to influence over key policy decision of all kinds. The European Parliament has extremely limited powers in the EU structure, and most citizens of member states would have difficulty in naming their own Member of the European Parliament (MEP).

A fundamental problem facing the EU is the democratic deficit reflected in the huge gap between the members of the European integrationist elite and the average citizen in the member states. The public increasingly resent the fact that they have such limited power to influence EU decisions and policy making. The real centres of power in the EU are to be found in the Council of Ministers appointed directly by the national governments and the European Commission, the EU's powerful bureaucracy which proposes and helps to decide central questions of policy in consultation with the Council of Ministers. It is true that the Commission also reports to and consults with the European Parliament, but although the Parliament is the only EU institution directly elected by EU citizens it has very limited legislative powers. Its most significant power is its right to approve or reject the EU budget. The EU is still an IGO with an elected consultative chamber, not a democratic superstate in embryo.

In view of the strong national loyalties of the leaders, legislators, and voters in the EU member states and their often conflicting perceptions of their national interest, is it no surprise that the EU's Common Foreign and Security Policy (CFSP) has been slow to develop and that European politicians have often expressed their frustration that the EU governments have been unable to agree on how to respond to major crises. For example, the Belgian Foreign Minister, Mark Eysken, impatient about the EU's lack of responsiveness during the 1991 Persian Gulf War, described Europe as 'an economic giant, a political dwarf and a military worm'. His comments show a fundamental failure to understand the nature of the EU project. The EU is not a truly autonomous actor in international affairs. Its external relations inevitably reflect the fact that its member states are not prepared to give up their sovereign control over their foreign policy. Moreover, as I have already observed, the EU states have never felt the need to make the organization into a powerful military alliance. They already have NATO to undertake that task. However, it is a serious mistake to dismiss the EU as a 'political dwarf': a label of this disparaging kind implies that the EU is a kind of sovereign state. In reality it is a potentially valuable mechanism for multilateral communication and cooperation on a daily basis. When the EU governments can agree on a common position on a major foreign-policy issue, as they did, for example, on how to respond to Iran's successful uranium enrichment, this provides EU political leaders with considerable additional diplomatic leverage. It has not escaped the notice of other states that the EU is an economic giant. It is the biggest and richest single consumer market in the world and, partly as a result of the EU's huge enlargement, the EU's total GDP and population are far greater than those of the North American Free Trade Area. Of course it is also the case that the EU's ability to influence international relations will be crucially affected by the political will of the governments of the member states and by the powers of persuasion of the EU's political leadership and top officials. The qualities of *statesmanship* which make a great difference to the fate of states are just as essential to the work of an IGO if it is going to attain any real influence on international relations and events. Another factor which can have a major effect on the opportunities of the EU to exercise real influence is the pressure of events and shifts in the global balance of power. The EU has a special window of opportunity to exert diplomatic leverage for its member states with the US government increasingly confronted by the high costs and risks of unilateral policies. In the midst of President George W. Bush's second term, after years of war in Iraq and with the particularly thorny problem of Iran's nuclear programme to deal with, it was clear in mid-May 2006 that the US was prepared to wait to see the results of multilateral diplomatic efforts, led by Javier Solana, the EU's foreign-policy chief, to find a peaceful resolution to the crisis. What the EU states acting in concert can bring to bear in such crises is what Professor Joseph S. Nye of Harvard University has termed 'soft power', the civilian sources of influence and peaceful persuasion such as economic strengths, diplomatic sophistication, and a reputation for fairness and objectivity. Above all, at a time when the policies and actions of the sole remaining superpower are provoking widespread anti-Americanism, it may be a huge advantage to have diplomatic initiatives which are clearly seen to be independent of those of the United States, even though they will need US willingness to accept the outcomes if they are going to work.

To sum up my conclusions on the roles of the United Nations and the European Union: (i) it would be a mistake to assume that these IGOs are truly autonomous actors in international relations; (ii) however, on behalf of their member states, they can at times exert considerable influence.

Some other regional IGOs

The Association of South East Asian Nations (ASEAN) was founded in 1967, after the Bangkok Declaration by Thailand, Singapore, Indonesia, the Philippines, and Malaysia. Brunei joined ASEAN in 1984 and Vietnam in 1995. It aims to promote regional economic, social, and cultural cooperation. The ASEAN economies have demonstrated a great potential for rapid economic growth. Singapore is usually regarded as one of the Asian 'Tiger' economies, exemplifying the benefits of economic liberalism, while Malaysia, Thailand, and Indonesia have been viewed as emerging 'Tiger' economies. The reason for the exclusion of China and Japan was the desire to ensure that the ASEAN economies were not dominated by the big economies of East Asia. ASEAN sees its role as being a counterweight to these major powers and to the United States.

ASEAN has a secretariat and has made progress in regional cooperation, especially in the economic field. It has not made any significant advances in regional military and security matters. ASEAN led the ASEAN Regional Forum initiative which involves cooperation with the EU and the Asia-Pacific Economic Cooperation countries (APEC). Although the economies of Indonesia and Thailand were severely affected by the tsunami in 2004, the ASEAN grouping continues to show great economic dynamism and has scope for enlargement by admitting other South East Asian countries.

Other regional IGOs of note are the Council of Arab Economic Unity (CAEU), founded in 1964 to promote economic integration among a dozen Arab states; the Caribbean Community and Common Market (CARICOM), which aims to develop integration and promote economic development among Caribbean countries; the Economic Community of West African States (ECOWAS), founded in 1975 to promote regional economic cooperation among 17 member states; the South Asian Association for Regional Cooperation (SAARC), founded in 1985 to promote economic, social, and cultural cooperation among South Asian States; and the Southern African Development Community (SADC), founded in 1992 to promote economic, social, and cultural cooperation between Southern African States.

None of the IGOs listed above is anywhere near as far advanced down the route of regional economic integration as the EU. However, they all have the potential to serve as useful mechanisms for strengthening economic development in their respective regions. As with the EU and other IGOs much will depend on the quality of the political leadership and the political will of their member states.

The Commonwealth

The final example of an IGO I shall briefly examine is the most unusual of all. It is not a regional IGO. The Commonwealth is a voluntary organization of 53 states, no less than 25 per cent of the states in the international system. Most, but not all, were formerly under the rule of the British Empire. It is the second largest IGO in the world and includes states from every region of the world except the Middle East. The Queen is the Head of the Commonwealth, although the organization includes republics, such as India, as well as countries which continue to recognize the Queen as their monarch. Conferences of the Commonwealth Heads of Government are held every two years, and all decisions are reached through consensus. Decisions to admit new member states have to be unanimous. It is obvious that the Commonwealth is not a power bloc. It is held together largely by shared values and by the desire to maintain this voluntary link with Britain and with other Commonwealth states. In addition, the Commonwealth provides a channel for obtaining additional technical assistance, training, and education resources. As one who has had the privilege of working as an adviser on one of the Commonwealth's major education projects, I am greatly impressed by the value of the scheme involved and the new possibilities it opens up for young people to change their lives by acquiring both new knowledge and a greater understanding of totally different cultures and political, social, and economic problems. The Commonwealth is above all about people power and discovering shared values as well as 'capacity-building' in the wider sense.

Chapter 4
Problems and challenges

In earlier chapters I have concentrated on providing the reader
with a guide to the main actors in international relations, their
roles, and their relative influence. It is now time to switch our
attention to some of the key problems and challenges which
confront the whole international community or large parts of
it. I should add that I am excluding national disasters which do
not result from human actions, such as earthquakes, volcanic
eruptions, and the devastating tsunami of December 2004 which
killed an estimated 150,000 people. It is true that in the case of
the Indian Ocean tsunami very large numbers of deaths could
have been avoided if there had been a sophisticated tsunami
warning system of the kind that covers the Pacific. It is also
true that much could have been done to improve the speed and
coordination of international humanitarian assistance in such
natural disasters. However, all the problems and challenges I
shall be briefly surveying result, whether by accident or design,
from human activity, and because of this it is at least theoretically
possible that by changing some aspects of human behaviour we
might succeed in considerably reducing or at least in mitigating
the problem.

I have chosen to focus on global issues not because I can offer
any easy solutions but because even a brief overview reveals the
huge complexity of the challenges and the difficulties facing

policy makers in their efforts to tackle them. Moreover, we should remember that our political leaders face some or all of these problems simultaneously. Given that resources are finite, how do we decide which problems require the highest priority? Perhaps without fully realizing it, our political leaders are often forced back into operating a kind of triage policy based purely on the basis of expedience. Should decisions about priorities be made on the basis of certain moral principles? If so, who is to make the ultimate decision? Which moral principles are to be employed, and on whose authority? And to whom, if anybody, are the decision makers to be held accountable? It would be foolish to underestimate the difficulties that arise for all those involved in the real world pressures of policy making, decision making, and crisis management.

In view of the intractability of the problems I am about to consider, it ill becomes academic specialists to sidestep the tough normative and policy issues involved. I have been greatly encouraged to find that the university students I have been privileged to teach find the normative and policy issues the most intellectually demanding and absorbing aspects of our subject. The reader should not be surprised to find that there will be a brief review of the search for solutions in the discussion of each of the major challenges to the international community.

The threat to environmental security from global warming

When the sun's heat reaches Earth a mixture of gases surrounding our planet acts as a filter. This layer of gases acts rather like glass in a greenhouse, with the result that it prevents too much heat getting through and too much heat escaping. Scientists of the Intergovernmental Panel on Climate Change (IPCC) – another IGO – have concluded that an increase in these 'greenhouse gases' is leading to too much heat being trapped near the earth's surface. They have termed this phenomenon 'global warming'.

The vast majority of scientists engaged in the study of the world's climate agree with the IPCC's conclusion that global warming is happening, that the most important of the gases which are intensifying the 'greenhouse effect' is carbon dioxide (CO_2), and that the major cause of global warming is the enormous increase in carbon emissions which have resulted from human activity such as the burning of fossil fuels by heavy industry, emissions from aircraft and motor vehicles, power stations, and domestic heating systems.

The countries responsible for most of these carbon emissions in the past were those which experienced the industrial revolution in the late 18th and 19th centuries and which have been contributing massively to the build-up of greenhouse gases ever since. However, today we are witnessing the very rapid industrialization of developing countries. For example, China, which has a population of over one and a quarter billion, relies on coal for 75 per cent of its energy resources. India, also with a population of over one billion, is going down a similar route of rapid industrial expansion, inevitably involving the burning of huge amounts of fossil fuels. Yet, how can the developed countries expect countries such as China and India to put a brake on the economic growth they so badly need to support their huge and rapidly growing populations?

It is even harder for the older industrial countries of the West to ask countries such as China and India to reduce their greenhouse gas emissions when the richest and biggest economy in the world, the US, is responsible for around 50 per cent of the world's carbon emissions and when the Bush administration has rejected the commitments made in the Kyoto Protocol (1997), when political leaders agreed to cut average CO_2 emissions by 5.2 per cent of 1990 levels by 2010. European countries agreed to reduce their emissions by 8 per cent, while President Clinton agreed that the US would cut emissions by 7 per cent. President Clinton was clearly convinced that greenhouse gases were responsible for global warming. President Bush and his advisers, at least in their first administration, were not convinced that the climate scientists were right about global warming. There was a belief among some right-wing Republicans that the Kyoto proposals to cut carbon emissions were the result of a conspiracy by environmentalists to damage the US economy. There have been serious allegations by the US climate scientists that the government edited, delayed, and in some cases suppressed reports that would have alerted the American people to the reality of global warming, but did not suit the Bush administration's political and electoral agenda.

The attempt to deny that global warming was taking place was curiously out of step with the more conventional US respect for science and technology. There has been an enormous investment into research into climate change, especially in US institutes and universities. The climate scientists have access to satellites which bring them an impressive amount of data that was never previously available, for example, on the changes in the upper atmosphere. They also have the benefits of sophisticated computer modelling. Yet some of the hostile and dismissive comments from powerful individuals in the US political and business elites seemed to imply that the climate scientists were relying on using astrology or pieces of seaweed to try to predict climate change. One is forced to conclude that the real reasons for attempts to discredit global warming research have had more to do with the fears of the energy industry, especially the oil majors, that their commercial interests would be harmed if the US government decided to back the implementation of tough controls on CO_2 emissions.

It is a matter of record that scientists had the data to prove that global warming was a reality over a decade ago. The IPCC had discovered in the mid-1990s temperatures rising faster than at any period in the previous 10,000 years, and they found that the Arctic temperatures were rising three to five times more rapidly than in any other part of the world. Scientists have predicted that within 50 years the Arctic ice cap will disappear entirely in the summer. And in the Antarctic scientists have found that the Larsen B ice shelf is melting and being broken up. This is a significant piece of evidence about global warming and its effects. The scientists tell us that since the Second World War temperatures in the Antarctic have risen by 2.5 per cent. Glaciers in the world's major mountain ranges are shrinking. According to the IPCC sea-levels have risen by 15 cm in the last century. They warn that there could be an additional increase of 18 cm by 2030, which could threaten millions living in low-lying coastal areas such as Tokyo, London, and New York, as well as people living in places like Bangladesh, the Maldives, and the South Pacific Islands which are only just above sea-level.

The search for solutions

The first really significant effort to mobilize international cooperation to help to combat human-induced global warming was an agreement at the UN Conference on Environment and Development (1992) held at Rio de Janeiro. The result, however, was very modest: 160 countries signed up to an agreement on promoting energy efficiency. The Kyoto conference (1997) was far more ambitious because it tried to get agreement on targets for reductions in greenhouse gases. Unfortunately the US pulled out altogether and many countries have failed to enforce the agreement through their national laws. It is now in any case all very academic because even if all countries, including the US, put the Kyoto Protocol into effect this would only make a minute difference to the quantity of CO_2 emissions. However, the Kyoto Protocol did contain one very imaginative feature. It enabled richer countries to buy the CO_2 allowances of other countries by means of a system of tradable permits. This could make it possible for those with very high levels of emissions to escape the need to make any cuts in gas emissions.

When one considers the potentially catastrophic effects of climate change for the whole planet it is very disappointing that there has been very little progress towards creating an international regime to regulate carbon emissions. The lack of leadership displayed by the world's only superpower has been disastrous: one can only hope that the swing back to greater use of multilateralism in US foreign policy means that the US government will try to give a real push to get an environmental security regime up and running. After the terrible damage from Hurricane Katrina to New Orleans and surrounding areas the White House must realize the dangers of neglecting the climate issue.

However, even if progress on an effective international regime is temporarily blocked, there are other measures that can be taken by national governments:

Governments could act to regulate deforestation, and to plant more trees. (Trees are an important means of absorbing CO_2.)

Richer countries could finance the acquisition of adequate expertise, technology, and training by developing countries.

We can save scarce energy resources by introducing greater efficiency in our homes, workplaces, and vehicles.

Local authorities, home owners, and businesses could make a big contribution collectively by switching from fossil fuels to renewables and should be given incentives to do so, such as receiving payment for the initial costs of the renewable technology and its installation.

Civil aviation is the fastest-growing and most polluting method of transport. Air travel is expected to grow by 50 per cent in the next ten years. Measures are needed to reduce the number of flights and to improve the fuel efficiency of aircraft engines. Central regulation to streamline the numbers/ destinations of airline flights would have the side benefit of reducing the strain on the airport and air traffic control facilities.

The above suggestions may seem rather obvious common sense, but although they lack the diplomatic glamour of an international agreement, *in combination* they could make a big impact in increasing environmental security.

Nuclear weapons

Any good introduction to international relations written in the second half of the 20th century would place the challenge of nuclear weapons, their proliferation, and the dangers involved in their possible use at the very top of the list of problems facing the international community. Today, in this age of environmental disasters, concerns about the effects of global warming, and international terrorism, it may seem to some readers unnecessarily gloomy to include them as a continuing problem for the international community. However, from the outset I have emphasized that I wished to provide an introduction to the *real* world of international relations, not the world as we might prefer it to be.

The harsh reality is that, despite the ending of the cold war and the efforts to develop an effective Nuclear Non-Proliferation Treaty regime, of which more later, we live in a world where nuclear weapon states still possess between them thousands of nuclear warheads. Moreover, according to the International Atomic Energy Agency, there are at least 40 additional states with civilian nuclear weapons development programmes ready in a matter of months. Among the states which have managed to develop a nuclear weapons development programme is North Korea, named as one of the 'Axis of Evil' states by President George W. Bush. Moreover, despite the denials by the Iranian government, it is widely believed that the Tehran regime is going to follow up its success in uranium enrichment by developing nuclear weapons.

Why do nuclear weapons cause such concern? They are not simply bigger equivalents of conventional bombs. It is true that the way

14. Hiroshima after the Allies dropped an atomic bomb on the city
(6 August 1945). Three days later an atomic bomb was dropped on
Nagasaki. Both cities were almost entirely destroyed and over 200,000
inhabitants were killed.

that nuclear weapons are described (that is, in the 'kiloton' or
megaton range) is a measurement of the amount of TNT which
would be required by a conventional weapon to approximate
to the explosive force of a nuclear weapon, but this does not
remotely capture the truly horrific nature of the effects of nuclear
weapons. The evidence we have on the impact of nuclear bombs
dropped on cities comes from the atom bomb attacks on the
Japanese cities of Hiroshima and Nagasaki on 6 and 9 August
1945 respectively. It is important to note that these atomic bombs
were very small compared to modern nuclear weapons in the
megaton range. Bruce Roth in his powerful work *No Time to Kill*
draws attention to the vivid observation by Carl Sagan: 'Modern
thermonuclear warheads use something like the Hiroshima bomb
as a trigger – the "match" to light the fusion action.'

Yet the bombing of Hiroshima and Nagasaki had effects which brought to reality the ghastly visions of hell which had been portrayed by the painter Hieronymus Bosch. The blasts killed an estimated 200,000 people. The Hiroshima bomb killed 50 per cent of the population in an area of three square miles around the epicentre of the bombing. The suffering of those who survived the first few hours or days of the attack was truly appalling.

Many survivors were found with pieces of skin hanging from them, so that their bones could be seen underneath. Many died from the terrible burns caused by the fireball. The heat from the fireball was so intense that people in the immediate vicinity of the epicentre were literally vaporized. Those who survived the initial blast but suffered from exposure to intense radiation experienced painful slow death. Bruce Roth describes the effects calmly and factually in *No Time to Kill*:

> Depending on the amount of radiation exposure, unlucky survivors of the initial blast develop mouth ulcers and purple spots on their skin from blood leaking out of their cells … They suffer nausea, diarrhoea, anaemia and internal bleeding as well as bleeding from the gums and from bodily orifices. Their hair falls out in clumps. Loss of white blood cells and antibodies lower their resistance to infection.

And, describing the fate of longer-term survivors, Roth observes:

> Anyone still alive either dies painfully over the next few weeks or prematurely from genetic damage leading to cancer and leukaemia. Many endure the remainder of their life with grotesque deformities.

Most historians of the Second World War agree that the decision to drop the atom bomb on Hiroshima was motivated by the desire of the US government to force Japan to surrender immediately, so that US troops would not have to face an opposed invasion on

Japan. It is also clear that the US government wanted to achieve this before the Soviet Union joined the war against Japan; there was a determination not to allow the Soviets to establish a sphere of influence over all or part of Japan. It does seem very clear from historical record that the Japanese government's decision to surrender unconditionally was heavily influenced by the atom bomb attacks. The decision to use the new weapon against Nagasaki has caused major controversy among ethicists as well as strategists. It could be argued that the bombing of Hiroshima was a 'test' for the use of the new weapon and that it demonstrated to the Japanese government the awesome power of these devices. Why, then, was there any need to use an atom bomb to attack Nagasaki only three days later?

The possible effects of an attack using a strategic nuclear warhead in the two megaton range can scarcely be imagined. Two megatons is roughly equivalent to the explosive force of the *total* number of bombs exploded in the Second World War, that is two million tons of TNT. But in addition to the effect of the initial blast and the shock wave caused there are also the impacts of the fireball (estimated temperature equivalent to that of the sun's surface), a huge electromagnetic pulse (EMP) big enough to disable all the micro circuits used in electronic equipment of all kinds, radioactive fallout, and climatic disruption.

The results of a single nuclear explosion in the one megaton range would include radioactive fallout being blown into the atmosphere. We can only try to imagine the effects of a number of nuclear weapons in the megaton range if they had been used in a major nuclear war between the superpowers in the 1970s or 1980s. A number of nuclear physicists developed a highly credible hypothesis or scenario of the likely effects on the planet's climate. They called it a 'nuclear winter', in which the dust and smoke blown into the atmosphere by the series of nuclear explosions would blot out the sun's rays, causing a dramatic reduction of temperature on the earth's surface.

Climate change of this catastrophic nature would undoubtedly affect whole populations and their food supply. Quite apart from the soil that would be virtually permanently poisoned by radioisotopes such as Uranium-235 with huge half-lives (the time it takes for half of the atoms to decay into other elements), there would be huge destruction of plants and animals. The survivors of the nuclear weapon attacks would not have sufficient supplies of food and drinking water. In brief, the decision by a government to launch into a major nuclear war would be equivalent to civilization as we know it committing suicide. With modern nuclear weapons, some of which are in the *200 megaton* range, a nuclear war has become the means by which political leaders with their fingers on the button could (probably unwittingly) be starting the slide to the annihilation of humanity.

It should be obvious from the above that the whole international community has a collective interest in more effective policies and measures to prevent the proliferation of nuclear weapons and to promote eventual general and complete nuclear disarmament.

There are two major types of proliferation: *vertical*, in which nuclear weapon states enhance their own and possibly their allies' nuclear armouries by developing even more powerful and accurate nuclear weapons and delivery systems through research and development, and *horizontal*, in which more and more states acquire nuclear weapons. Despite the well-intentioned efforts of those who designed the existing Nuclear Non-Proliferation Treaty regime and those who are now charged with the responsibility of making it work, both kinds of proliferation are continuing.

The search for solutions

Once the nuclear weapon had been invented it was inevitable that the Soviet Union and other states would acquire their own. It is simply unrealistic to assume that the whole international community of states can immediately agree to general and complete nuclear disarmament, however powerful the anti-nuclear weapons protests by public campaigns for nuclear disarmament and the urgings of UN officials and religious leaders. Governments of the nuclear weapon states clearly do not trust each other sufficiently to take such a radical step. Their leaders believe (in my view with a powerful strategic logic to support their position) that possession of a viable nuclear deterrent, that is a nuclear weapon which would survive a first strike by an aggressor, is vital for their national security. Governments of nuclear weapon states would also argue that, given the absence of a world sovereign body capable of enforcing international agreement, there is always the danger that one or more states would fail to honour a nuclear disarmament treaty and this carries the risk that the 'rogue' state or states would then be able to blackmail non-nuclear weapon states by threatening them with nuclear attack.

Recognition of the essential intractability of this central problem of modern international relations, and the belief that deterrence can be harnessed as a positive contribution to international security and diplomacy underpin the arms control approach, both to nuclear weapons proliferation and the dangers posed by the proliferation of chemical and biological weapons, and new types of conventional weapons. The basic philosophy of the arms control approach is that, while general disarmament is not a feasible policy objective in our current international system, it is still possible to obtain workable agreements on *limiting* or *restraining* both vertical and horizontal weapons proliferation, and other military capabilities. This is obviously a very different approach from that pursued by the supporters of comprehensive disarmament. What unites both arms controllers and disarmers, however, is the conviction that an uncontrolled arms race in this age of weapons of mass destruction would lead to disaster for the whole community.

One of the proudest achievements of the arms control approach during the cold war was the drafting and ratification of the Treaty on the Non-Proliferation of Nuclear Weapons, opened for signature in July 1968 and brought into force in March 1970.

The key objectives of the Non-Proliferation Treaty were:

to stop the horizontal proliferation of nuclear weapons;

to limit or restrain the process of vertical proliferation by urging signatory states to negotiate on effective measures to end the nuclear arms race at an early date, and on nuclear disarmament; and

to establish an international regime which permits the safe transfer of civil nuclear power technology, with the International Atomic Energy Agency (IAEA) policing a safeguards system in which the IAEA would have full and open access to the civilian nuclear programmes of all non-nuclear weapon states, including the right to periodically inspect their civil nuclear plants and facilities.

One of the major criticisms of the Non-Proliferation Treaty is that it gives a privileged status to those powers which are already in possession of nuclear weapons. Although the 1995 review conference agreed to extend the Non-Proliferation Treaty indefinitely, the fact is that the weaknesses of the Non-Proliferation Treaty regime have become more glaringly apparent in recent years. Undoubtedly the most serious of flaws in the Non-Proliferation Treaty is its failure to ensure that the US and other nuclear weapons states live up to their commitments to seek to end the nuclear arms race. The US as the only remaining superpower should be seen to be taking the lead in this aspect of the Treaty. In reality it has gone into reverse. It has embarked on a costly programme to develop a new generation of nuclear weapons with additional capabilities.

The Bush administration withdrew from the Anti-Ballistic Missile Treaty in December 2001, thus opening the way to an arms race in outer space, now well under way. It is also known that the US has been developing underground nuclear testing sites in Nevada, in clear violation of its commitments under the Comprehensive Test Ban Treaty, and has been maintaining tactical nuclear weapons at bases in Europe in clear violation of a pledge made at the 2000 Non-Proliferation Treaty Review Conference.

The US is not the only nuclear weapons state which is violating its Non-Proliferation Treaty commitments. Russia is already embarked on a programme of rearmament and a major extension of its anti-ballistic defences. It seems hardly necessary to point out that when the major nuclear weapons states are flagrantly defying the provisions of the Non-Proliferation Treaty it undermines efforts to persuade other states to ratify that Treaty and to dissuade some states from going ahead with secret nuclear weapon development.

In view of these serious flaws in the Non-Proliferation Treaty, what is to be done? Complete nuclear disarmament is not a practicable proposition in the current state of international relations. At the extreme, an uncontrolled nuclear arms race would be extremely dangerous, greatly increasing the danger of a nuclear war, either by accident or design. We need to remember that the end of the cold war did not remove the danger of a nuclear war. There is a real possibility that a conventional war between two nuclear weapons states could escalate to a nuclear war. It is also possible that in a war in which another weapon of mass destruction has been used a nuclear strike could be launched by one of the belligerents.

Another plausible scenario would be a massive terrorist attack, possibly involving WMD, leading to the targeted state responding with a nuclear attack on a state believed to sponsor the terrorists. In the extraordinarily difficult search for solutions it would be absurd to claim that there are any easy routes to tackling the problem of nuclear weapons proliferation and the dangers of nuclear war.

However, I suggest that it would be irresponsible to discard or neglect the arms control route to reducing the dangers. This was the clear conclusion of the experts of the independent Weapons of Mass Destruction Commission (WMDC), chaired by Dr Hans Blix, which published its report in the summer of 2006.

There is no space here to summarise all the Commission's recommendations. However, it is very clear that the main

WMDC recommendations

All parties to the Non-Proliferation Treaty need to revert to the fundamental and balanced non-proliferation and disarmament commitments that were made under the treaty and confirmed in 1995 when the treaty was extended indefinitely.

All parties to the Non-Proliferation Treaty should implement the decision on principles and objectives for non-proliferation and disarmament, the decision on strengthening the Non-Proliferation Treaty review process, and the resolution on the Middle East as a zone free of nuclear and all other weapons of mass destruction, all adopted in 1995. They should also promote the implementation of the 'thirteen practical steps' for nuclear disarmament that were adopted in 2000.

To enhance the effectiveness of the nuclear non-proliferation regime, all Non-Proliferation Treaty non-nuclear-weapon states parties should accept comprehensive safeguards as strengthened by the International Atomic Energy Agency Additional Protocol.

conclusion of this team of the top arms control experts in the world is that the international community simply cannot afford to allow the achievements of the Non-Proliferation Treaty and the Comprehensive Test Ban Treaty regimes to sink under the sand of political neglect and hypocrisy. They call urgently upon all parties to the Non-Proliferation Treaty to rededicate themselves to the principles and objectives of the Non-Proliferation Treaty and the pledges they made in the original agreement and in successive review conferences. The three major initial recommendations of the Commission's report, regarding nuclear weapon proliferation, clearly underline the importance of the maintenance and strengthening of the Non-Proliferation Treaty regime, and of adapting arms control diplomacy to the challenges currently intensifying in the Middle East and elsewhere.

Chemical and biological weapons

Chemical and Biological Warfare (CBW) weapons are far more accessible and low-cost than nuclear weapons and yet also have the capacity to kill thousands of people. Biological weapons consist of bacteria, viruses, and rickettsiae and include inhaled anthrax, coetaneous anthrax, the Plague, Ebola, Lassa fever, and botulism. Anthrax was sent through the US Postal Service in the United States in October 2001. It killed five people and severely poisoned 22. By far the most lethal of all the toxins that could be used is botulinum toxin. Scientists claim that a single gram of this toxin, especially when used in enclosed areas or to contaminate food and water supply, could, if evenly dispersed and inhaled, kill up to a million people.

There are three major types of chemical weapons: poison gases, incapacitants, and anti-plant agents. It is well known that Saddam Hussein used a gas against the Kurds in Halabja, Iraq on 16 March 1988. Five thousand people were killed, most of whom were women and children. Mustard gas was used by both sides in the First World War. It is believed that Saddam Hussein's forces used mustard gas, VX nerve gas, and cyanide during the Iraq–Iran War in the 1980s.

The search for solutions

The techniques of arms control have been deployed to develop the most comprehensive and intrusive international chemical weapons agreement ever signed, the Chemical Weapons Convention (CWC) in 1993. The CWC prohibits not just the first use of chemical weapons but *all* use of chemical weapons. It also bans the production, development, stockpiling, and transfer of chemical weapons, and enables the newly established Organization for the Prohibition of Chemical Weapons (OPCW) to monitor chemical plants and industrial sites around the world. The CWC inspection regime began work in 1996.

Unfortunately the Biological Weapons Convention (1972) does not contain the verification procedures that are so vital if it is to be truly effective. However, there have been considerable international efforts to apply some of the lessons that can be drawn from the CWC to the biological and toxin weapons areas, and there is now a need to mobilize universal support for and adherence to the new Biological and Toxin Weapons Convention.

I conclude by suggesting that, as in the nuclear weapons field, a real strengthening of arms control regimes is the sensible way to reduce the danger of weapons of mass destruction of all kinds. Once again, the reader is recommended to consult the expert report of the Independent Commission on Weapons of Mass Destruction. There is no space here to describe its ambitious set of recommendations. However, the major recommendations regarding both biological and toxin weapons and chemical weapons are quoted in the box over leaf.

It will require statesmanship and diplomacy of great skill to rejuvenate the arms control approach that was so cavalierly and

Expert recommendations on BCW weapons

Recommendation 31

All states not yet party to the Biological and Toxin Weapons Convention should adhere to the Convention. The states parties to the Convention should launch a campaign to achieve universal adherence by the time of the Seventh Review Conference to be held in 2011.

Recommendation 32

To achieve universal adoption of national legislation and regulations to implement the Biological and Toxin Weapons Convention completely and effectively, the states parties should offer technical assistance and promote best practice models of such legislation. As a part of the confidence-building process and to promote transparency and harmonization, all states should make annual biological-weapon-related national declarations and make them public.

Recommendation 33

States parties to the Biological and Toxin Weapons Convention should enhance the investigatory powers to the UN Secretary-General, ensuring that the Secretary-General's office can rely upon a regularly updated roster of experts and advice from the World Health Organisation and a specialist unit, modelled on the United Nations Monitoring, Verification and Inspection Committee, to assist in investigating unusual outbreaks of disease and allegations of the use of biological weapons.

Recommendation 34

States must prevent terrorists from gaining access to nuclear weapons or fissile material. To achieve this, they must maintain fully effective accounting and control of all stocks of fissile and radioactive materials and other radiological sources on their territories. They should ensure that there is personal legal responsibility for any acts of nuclear terrorism or activity in support of such terrorism. They must expand their cooperation through *inter alia* the sharing of information, including intelligence on illicit nuclear commerce. They should also promote universal adherence to the International Convention for the Suppression of Acts of Nuclear Terrorism and the Convention on the Physical Protection of Nuclear Material and implementation of UN Security Council Resolution 1540.

foolishly cast aside by the US and UK governments in the lead up to the Iraq War in 2002–3. It is worth bearing in mind that if Dr Hans Blix had been given time to complete the rigorous weapons inspection he was leading in Iraq, the prolonged war in Iraq which has cost so many thousands of lives could have been avoided.

15. The bombing of Baghdad in March 2003 during Operation Shock and Awe.

Effective arms control and crisis management (which is actually a key part of arms control) are *not* appeasement: they are a way, probably the only practicable way, of preventing, dampening down and managing conflict in a dangerous world of many states still armed with weapons of mass destruction.

Preventing genocide and other violations of human rights

The term genocide originated in the 20th century. Although the phenomenon occurred in previous centuries, the last century could truly be called the Age of Genocide and 'ethnic cleansing',

16. Victims of the Holocaust, the mass murder of Jews in continental Europe by the Nazis between 1940 and 1945. Six million died, the worst ever act of genocide.

which could more accurately be termed violence of a genocidal nature.

The UN Genocide Convention approved by the General Assembly in December 1948 defines genocide in Article 2 as an act of 'destroying, in whole or in part, a national, ethnical, racial or religious group', including killing, seriously injuring, or causing mental harm to members of such groups, inflicting upon such groups adverse living conditions so that the physical destruction of the group is threatened, deliberate attempts to prevent members of the group from having children, and forcibly transferring children from one group to another. Under the Convention conspiracy to commit genocide, incitement to commit genocide, and complicity in genocide are also punishable.

It is clear that the Convention was passed in response to the Holocaust, the attempt by the Nazi regime in Germany to exterminate the Jews in which six million Jews were taken to death camps and murdered. The Nuremberg trials were a catalyst for this ambitious effort to extend the international criminal law in a brave attempt to enable it to deal with the most horrendous mass violations of human rights, crimes against humanity.

The tragic reality is that the noble intentions of those who drafted the Convention have not been translated into effective action. The genocide committed by the Pol Pot regime in Cambodia, estimated to have cost around two million lives, could not be prevented or terminated by the international community. The same is true of the genocide of Rwanda. Intervention by the UN and NATO to stop genocidal violence in Bosnia and Kosovo was very belated, though ultimately highly effective, but it is clear that the UN acting alone would not have had the resources to implement the will of the Security Council.

At the time of writing (summer 2006) the weaknesses of the UN and other IGOs in dealing with the crisis in Sudan's Darfur region were once again being tragically demonstrated. Representatives of various governments who have visited the huge refugee camps in South and West Darfur and spoken to some of those who have been forced to flee from their homes and briefed themselves on the crises have described the violence committed against the African rural population by the Janjawid Arab militia, backed by the Sudanese government, as genocidal in character.

Over a quarter of a million people were forced out their homes. Many have been subjected to rape, murder, and looting by the Janjawid and it is estimated that well over 100,000 people have died in the attacks on civilians.

The crisis began in February 2003, when the Justice and Equality Movement and the Sudan Liberation Army started a rebellion against the Khartoum authorities in order to obtain political recognition and a larger share of Sudan's resources. The government's response was to arm and unleash the Janjawid Arab militia, though government officials have repeatedly denied all responsibility for Janjawid attacks. Three years later the UN had still been unable to take effective action other than to send humanitarian aid to the hard-pressed refugees. The major obstacle to getting Security Council agreement on sanctions against Sudan has been China, which as a permanent member can veto any such proposal. It is important to note that China has extensive commercial interests in Sudan and has repeatedly opposed UN intervention, even when the humanitarian case is overwhelming. Even the delivery of humanitarian aid has repeatedly been jeopardized by attacks on aid agency staff and by the looting of World Food Programme (WFP) trucks.

I have used the case of Darfur to underline the weakness of the international mechanisms for intervention to prevent or at least to stop the most serious mass violations of the basic human right, the right to life. However, let us not forget that there are many other cases where thousands are suffering from these problems. One only has to recall the sufferings of the civilian population in East Timor, Myanmar (formerly Burma), Liberia, Sierra Leone, and Togo – all current or recent examples where conflict has take a huge toll on human rights – to see the extent of the challenge.

The search for solutions

Although it is hard to find examples of significant improvement in the effective prevention of genocidal violence and major war crimes, there has been some modest progress towards finding international judicial measures and mechanisms to bring war criminals to justice. For example, The Hague Tribunal to deal with war crimes suspects from the conflict in the former Yugoslavia and the parallel Tribunal set up to deal with war crimes suspects from Rwanda have been very rigorous in their conduct of trials. The Hague Tribunal to deal with the former Yugoslavia was set up in 1993 and was in the process of conducting the trial of Slobodan Milosevic before his death from natural causes. This was the most important of all The Hague war crimes tribunal cases so far because this was the first time a former head of state had been put on trial to face charges of this kind.

It is hardly surprising that in the last century, characterized by the most terrible wars and mass violation of human rights in history, the international community struggled to find ways of bringing those guilty of war crimes to justice before their own courts. In many cases this proves impossible because the accused person/persons flee abroad. In other cases, for example in Serbia, the persons wanted for war crimes are sheltered by sympathizers who refuse to divulge their whereabouts. And in cases where, for example, a former dictator is put on trial before a court in his own state, it is by no means certain that the judicial system will be capable of dealing with the formidable complexities involved. The International War Crimes Tribunal at Nuremburg, which tried the main leadership of the Nazi regime, proved a highly effective

17. Guantanamo Bay is a US base in Cuba used as a prison for men suspected of involvement with Al Qaeda. The prisoners have been prevented from resort to US Federal courts and have no opportunity to prove their innocence.

way of bringing major war criminals to justice. Not surprisingly this judicial device has been found invaluable in dealing with mass violations of human rights in more recent conflicts.

Many people assumed that the most appropriate way of bring the former Iraqi dictator, Saddam Hussein, to justice was to let the Iraqi legal system deal with the case. The fact that Iraqi courts and judges had no previous experience or expertise in handling such cases was overlooked. A better solution might have been to set up a special international tribunal comprising judges with special qualifications and experience in handling international human rights law. An even better alternative might have been to hand over responsibility for the trial to the newly established International Criminal Court (ICC).

I have already noted that the International Criminal Tribunal for the former Yugoslavia (ICTY) provided a highly effective mechanism for bringing war criminals from Serbia, Croatia, and

Bosnia to justice. It is a matter of record that under the tough and determined leadership of the UN war crimes prosecutor, Carla Del Ponte, the tribunal achieved an impressive series of successful prosecutions. The success of ICTY was of course assisted by the strong backing of the US government.

A far more ambitious project, the International Criminal Court, is now at work. The Court proposal was the product of an international conference in Rome in 1998. By April 2002 the ICC project had obtained the necessary 60 ratifications from member states of the UN. The Court had a global remit to investigate war crimes and crimes against humanity, including crimes by a state against its own people.

This is a major innovation in international cooperation on human rights. It has been supported by almost all the major democracies except the US. This seems curiously out of keeping with Washington's enthusiastic support for the International Criminal Tribunal on the former Yugoslavia. The explanation given by the US ambassador for war crimes was that the US was concerned that the Court would have the power to try Americans, and that opponents of the US might order the arrest of US servicemen or political leaders, even perhaps the President himself. The absence of the world's only superpower is a significant weakness. Another weakness stems from the limited jurisdiction of the ICC. It can only try war crimes if they are committed by personnel of one of the ratifying parties to the court treaty, or in the territory of one of the state parties. There are now 97 state parties to the ICC treaty and there are an additional 42 who have signed but not yet ratified, including four permanent members of the Security Council. With such a lack of support from the major powers the ICC starts with a great handicap. Yet again I note the difficulty of getting concerted action by the international state system on even the most fundamental human rights problems. Human rights NGOs are lobbying hard to gain support for the ICC from the key democracies but as yet they have been unable to mobilize significant support from the general public or from the policy makers in the defaulting countries.

I, and I suspect many others, share the human rights organizations' sense of frustration and disappointment. In commenting on his own government's failure to ratify the ICC, Benjamin Ferencz, one of the prosecution team at Nuremberg and author of *An International Criminal Court: A Step Toward World Peace* observed:

> The United States has been misled by the right wing, the reactionary conservatives who are isolationist in sentiment, who are distorting the truth, and confusing the public ... At Nuremberg we were really the leader and we said the law we laid down would be the law we would follow tomorrow. Those ideals have been forgotten.

The North/South divide

One of the most intractable problems in international relations is the polarization between the Advanced Industrial Countries (AICs) of the Global North and the poverty-stricken Global South Less Developed Countries (LDCs). The typical *developed* state of the Global North is one where there is self-sustained economic growth in all industrial sectors – primary, secondary, and tertiary.

LDCs are, in contrast, characterized by low GDP, low *per capita* GDP, low *per capita* growth and low life expectancy combined with high population growth rates. A third group, the Newly Industrializing Countries (NICs) of which key examples are South Korea, Taiwan, Singapore, and Hong Kong, have sometimes been termed the 'Tiger' economies because of their swift industrial expansions and their success in achieving export-led economic growth. There are clearly some special factors which explain the rise of the NICs in Asia. They have managed to exploit the advantages of having lower labour costs than the AICs and they combine this with a highly competitive liberal economic system. (In contrast they tend to have authoritarian political systems but this does not appear to impede their economic development.) NICs have also been able to gain great advantage from their enthusiastic readiness to accept foreign investment and from the natural business skills that appear to be available within their populations. The success of the 'Tiger' economies is borne out by the economic statistics for 2006 which show, for example, Hong Kong with a higher *per capita* GDP than Germany, Canada, Belgium, and France; and Singapore with a higher *per capita* GDP than Australia and Italy. Hong Kong, Singapore, and Taiwan are in the top 20 per cent of countries with the highest purchasing power. Even more striking is the fact Hong Kong and Singapore come first and second respectively in the economic freedom index calculated on the basis of ten indicators of how government intervention can restrict the economic relations between individuals. Singapore, Malaysia, South Korea, and Taiwan were all in the top 10 per cent of countries with the highest economic growth, 1991–2001.

In stark contrast, the poorest of the Least Developed Countries appear to be caught in a permanent state of immiseration. No less than 16 of the 20 countries with the lowest GDP per head are in Africa. Many LDCs have negative annual growth rates of *per capita* income. Demographers estimate that the world population will grow from its current (2006) total of over six billion to between 10 and 12 billion in 2050, depending on whether world fertility will continue to decline. Whatever the final future, most experts are certain that the world population will continue to grow during this century and well into the 22nd. There is also wide agreement that the most rapid growth will be in the Global South. This is because, in addition to high birth rates and falling death rates, the Global South is going to experience *population momentum* due to the large number of women now arriving at childbearing age and this seems set to continue despite the AIDS pandemic which has hit Africa and other parts of the

Global South. (I have taken AIDS into account in my estimate of the population growth rate.) Roughly 70 per cent of those infected with AIDS live in Africa as compared with South and South-East Asia where, it is estimated, around six million are infected with AIDS. The economic effects of the AIDS pandemic have been nothing less than calamitous. The medical services in the worst affected African countries are simply unable to cope and, because the majority of victims are young or middle aged, the effect on economic performance is devastating as families can no longer support themselves, produce food, or care for their relatives.

The third major factor threatening the very survival of the civilian population of many areas in the Global South is the effect of conflict. For example, in Africa, over 30 per cent of countries have experienced particularly lethal wars which have driven people out of their farms and villages. Last but not least, the plight of the Global South countries has been made infinitely worse by environmental disasters such as drought, desertification, and deforestation.

The process of globalization which enables financial and investment markets to operate internationally, mainly as a result of deregulation and improved communications, and which allows companies to expand and operate internationally, have not had the result of narrowing the gap between the AICs of the Global North and the LDCs of the Global South. On the contrary, the main effect has been to make the Global North states richer, because when they do choose to locate manufacturing plants in LDCs, the profit from these enterprises mainly benefits the Global North. Some commentators choose to stress the alleged advantages of 'interdependence' to the LDCs. In reality only those LDCs which produce commodities which are in high demand in the AICs, such as oil and natural gas, are likely to become beneficiaries of globalization. The rest of the LDCs have become more and more dependent on aid because if they were to rely solely on the production of a simple agricultural produce, such as coffee or bananas, they would simply remain in the poverty trap forever. Moreover, if the LDCs are dependent on exports of agricultural produce to the Global North they will find that they are confronted with protectionist trade measures of the rich states, such as tariff barriers and quotas. It was hoped that the World Trade Organization talks of 2006 would find ways of considerably reducing these obstacles, which in effect prevent LDCs from benefiting from the world trade system, but at the time of writing there was no significant breakthrough in sight.

The Gleneagles 2005 Agreement of the G8 Ministers to write off very large amounts of LDC debt is certainly a welcome relief. UK Chancellor of the Exchequer, Gordon Brown, and his colleagues and the 'Make Poverty History' NGO campaign can take some satisfaction from the G8 debt relief decisions. However, we need to recognize that this generous gesture is not going to address the fundamental causes of underdevelopment inherent in the international system.

The search for solutions

As is the case with the other major problems I have briefly reviewed, there is no simple solution to the problem of the widening gap between Global North and South. It is fair to say that there has been a serious shortage of well-informed strategic thinking about the challenges of international development in recent years. The last really serious effort at designing a comprehensive international development strategy was the work of the Independent Commission on International Development Issues, chaired by Former West German Chancellor, Willy Brandt, in the late 1970s. In 1980 they published their remarkable report, *North–South: A Programme for Survival*. The Brandt Report approach could aptly be described as international Keynesianism. Its underlying assumptions were based on economic liberalism modified to fit the special needs of the Global South. It argued that the world trade system needed to adjust its rules to enable the LDCs to gain a fair return on their exports. Brandt also argued that foreign aid should be targeted more carefully in order to assist recipients to become more economically self-sustainable, and to give more help to LDCs in capacity-building, for example, by providing technical expertise and training where this was unavailable through private sector investment. One of the Commission's most important conclusions was that NGOs in the international development field have a key role to play and that this should be recognized fully by governments so that they could cooperate in more effective partnerships internationally.

All these lessons are just as valid today, though a great deal has been done to improve international cooperation on development issues and the UN's specialized agencies have a particularly distinguished record in this field.

However, it would be grossly misleading, indeed dishonest, to pretend that all the potential partial solutions to the problem of underdevelopment are in the hands of the Global North and the IGOs. It is up to the political leaders, citizens, and legal systems of LDCs to root out the corruption and large-scale organized crime which often take place not just through government incompetence but with the connivance of the state authorities. Any report of serious malfeasance by officials, including the illegal diversion of aid, should be reported and thoroughly investigated, and the authorities should ensure that aid is distributed fairly and properly accounted for. Opponents of aid in donor countries will seize hold of any reports of maladministration to justify stopping aid altogether, however desperate the need.

Conclusion

It would be entirely understandable if the reader felt somewhat depressed at this stage in this short introduction. A brief survey of some of the major problems and challenges of international relations reveals that we live in a very dangerous world, and that many of the most serious threats to our peace, security, and economic and social well-being are the result of human actions.

The 'New World Order', which President George W. Bush's father hoped to usher in at the end of the cold war now appears to have been a hopelessly overoptimistic notion. Most sensible observers today realize that there are severe limits to what can be achieved by unilateral foreign policy initiatives. Big international changes such as the reform of the UN can only be achieved when there is agreement among the major powers. Even the reform of the EU has to be agreed by 25 member states.

One of the key lessons one can draw from the recent history of international relations is the importance of skilful, patient diplomacy, building cooperation not only with states but also with IGOs and non-state organizations. We should bear in mind that there have been huge achievements through peaceful diplomacy over the past half-century. Most of the day-to-day work of the Foreign and Commonwealth Office and our ambassadors abroad involves relations with states which are basically friendly and cooperative and whose governments abide by international agreements, conduct trade and diplomacy according to the rules, and so on.

This not only applies to small and medium-sized powers. The successive leaders of the world's sole superpower have learnt from experience that unilateralism does not work. There are limits to their power and influence and as they cannot control international relations, they have to rely on the diplomacy of multilateralists, including the imperfect yet indispensable UN.

It follows that in a world where states possess weapons of mass destruction, international statesmanship and leadership cannot be measured purely in terms of the use, or threat of use, of military power as a regular tool of foreign policy. Of course, in the last resort, when your national security is *genuinely* at risk, you must be prepared to use military force, but overdependence on military 'solutions' is highly dangerous and potentially counterproductive. Even a superpower cannot remake the entire international system in its own image. It has to learn to *manage* tensions and disputes and prevent conflict, because the risks of escalating inter-state conflict are so great that it is not in the national security interest to get dragged into so-called 'pre-emptive wars' against all the brutal undemocratic regimes in the world.

It is important to bear in mind that only a small minority of states have democratic political systems. The international system is very far from being a democracy. But that does not mean that our foreign policy should be conducted without reference to certain underlying principles.

I stressed earlier the vital contribution of outstanding international statesmen and national political leaders in resolving problems and challenges. What key principles should guide our current policy makers, parliaments, and publics in making foreign policy in a democracy? They should be, above all, committed to international peace and security, because without this we could so swiftly bring to an end human life on this planet. We should also expect them to be genuine internationalists with a commitment to serving the good of humanity and not simply a narrow national or sectional interest. They should seek to promote multi-religious and multi-ethnic tolerance not only within our democracies but also globally, through policies on human rights and development assistance to the Global South.

It goes almost without saying that they should be fully committed to upholding the basic rights and freedoms enshrined in such documents as the UN Declaration of Human Rights (1948) and the European Convention for the Protection of Human Rights and Fundamental Freedoms (1950).

Last but not least, we should expect our democratic political leaders to be committed to spreading the principles and practice of democratic governance and observance of the rule of law, while recognizing that this is inevitably a difficult task which needs to be pursued by example and quiet persuasion and not imposed by force. This is most accurately characterized as a liberal democratic response to the challenges and dangers which confront both democracies and undemocratic states in an international system of states which is now all too capable of destroying itself.

Further reading

Arendt, Hannah, *The Origins of Totalitarianism* (1958)

Aristotle, *Politics*, tr. Benjamin Jowett (1885)

Avirgan, Tony, and Honey, Martha, *War in Uganda, the Legacy of Idi Amin* (1982)

Baylis, John, and Smith, Steve, *The Globalization of World Politics*, 3rd edn (2006)

Black, George, Rone, Jemera, and Hitermann, Joost, *Middle East Watch: Genocide in Iraq. The Anfal Campaign Against the Kurds* (1993)

Bull, Hedley, *The Anarchical Society. A Study of Order in World Politics* (1977)

Carr, E. H., *Nationalism and After* (1945)

Carr, E. H., *What is History?* (1967)

Evans, Graham, and Newnham, Jeffrey, *The Penguin Dictionary of International Relations* (2006)

Ferencz, Benjamin, *An International Criminal Court: A Step towards World Peace*, 2 vols (1975)

Friedrich, Carl, and Brzezinski, Zbigniew, *Totalitarian Dictatorship and Autocracy* (1956)

Fukuyama, Francis, *After the Neocons: America at the Crossroads*, (2007)

Gilbert, Martin, *Recent History Atlas, 1860–1960* (1966)

Giraudoux, Jean, *Tiger at the Gates* (1935)

Grotius, Hugo, *De Jure Belli ac Pacis* (On the Law of War and Peace) (1625)

Hinsley, Francis Harry, *Power and the Pursuit of Peace: Theory and Practice in the History of Relations between States* (1963)

Independent Commission on International Development Issues, *North–South: A Programme for Survival* (1980)

Independent Commission on Weapons of Mass Destruction (chaired by Hans Blix), *Weapons of Terror Report* (2006); available online: http://www.wmdcommission.org

Jackson, R. H., *Quasi States: Sovereignty, International Relations and the Third World* (1990)

Jervis, Robert, *Perceptions and Misperceptions in International Politics* (1976)

Judt, Tony, *Postwar* (2005)

Kedourie, Elie, *Nationalism* (1960; repr. 2004)

Laqueur, Walter, *Guerrilla Warfare: A Historical and Critical Study* (1997)

Luard, Evan, *The United Nations: How it Works and What it Does* (1979)

McDowall, David, *A Modern History of the Kurds* (1996)

Machiavelli, Niccolo, *The Prince and the Discourses*, ed. Max Lerner (1950)

Mead, Margaret, *Coming of Age in Samoa* (1929)

Mill, John Stuart, *On Liberty* (1860)

Montevideo Convention on Rights and Duties of States, 1933

O'Kane, Rosemary, *Terrorism*, 2 vols (2006)

Orwell, George, *1984* (1949)

Pirouet, Louise M., *Historical Dictionary of Uganda* (1995)

Posen, Barry, 'The Security Dilemma and Ethnic Conflict', *Survival*, 35/1 (Spring 1993)

Rageau, Jean-Pierre, and Chaliand, Gérard, *A Strategic Atlas: Comparative Geopolitics of the World's Powers* (1990)

Roth, Bruce A., *No Time to Kill* (2006)

Solzhenitsyn, A., *The Gulag Archipelago* (1975)

Taber, Richard, *The War of the Flea* (1965)

Taylor, A. J. P., *The First World War* (1972)

The Economist, *The World in Figures* (2004)

Wilkinson, Paul, *Terrorism and the Liberal State*, 2nd edn (1986)

Wilkinson, Paul, *Terrorism Versus Democracy: The Liberal State Response*, 2nd edn (2006)

Index

Visit the
VERY SHORT
INTRODUCTIONS
Web site

www.oup.co.uk/vsi

➤ **Information** about all published titles

➤ News of **forthcoming books**

➤ **Extracts** from the books, including titles
not yet published

➤ **Reviews** and views

➤ **Links** to other **web sites** and main
OUP web page

➤ Information about **VSIs in translation**

➤ **Contact** the editors

➤ **Order** other **VSIs** on-line

THE EUROPEAN UNION
A Very Short Introduction
John Pinder

John Pinder writes with expert knowledge of the European
Union, explaining the interplay between governments and
federal elements in the institutions; consensus over the
single market and the environment; and conflicts over
agriculture, social policies, the Euro and frontier controls.
He shows how the Union relates to its European
neighbours, The United States, and the rest of the world,
and outlines the choices that lie ahead. He is clear about
his federalist orientation, presents the arguments fairly, and
is scrupulous about the facts. This is quite simply the best
short book on the subject.

> 'This short, detailed yet splendidly readable book . . . is a
> must for anyone seeking to understand the European
> Union, its origins, development, and possible future.'
>
> **Michael Palliser**

> '. . . indispensable not only for beginners but for all
> interested in European issues. Pithy, lucid, accessible it
> covers recent history, institutions, and policies, as well as
> future developments.'
>
> **Rt. Hon. Giles Radice, MP**

www.oup.co.uk/isbn/0-19-285375-9